Guide to OS/2

Allen G. Taylor

Scott, Foresman and Company
Glenview, Illinois   London

Trademarks

IBM is a registered trademark and PC-AT, PS/2, OS/2, PC-DOS are trademarks of International Business Machines Corporation

Matchmaker is a trademark of Dolphin Systems Technology

Microsoft is a registered trademark of Microsoft Corporation

8080, 8086, 8088, 80286, 80386 are trademarks of Intel Corporation

CP/M-80, CP/M-86 are trademarks of Digital Research Corporation

Z-80 is a trademark of Zilog Corporation

Compaq is a trademark of Compaq Computer Corporation

Zenith is a trademark of Zenith Corporation

PC Mouse is a trademark of Mouse Systems, Inc.

WordStar is a trademark of MicroPro International

WordPerfect is a trademark of WordPerfect Corp.

Library of Congress Cataloging-in-Publication Data

Taylor, Allen G.
  Guide to OS/2.

  Includes index.
  1. MS OS/2 (Computer operating system)
I. Title.   II. Title: Guide to operating system two.
QA76.76.063T386   1989   005.4'469   88-11483

1 2 3 4 5 6 KPF 93 92 91 90 89 88

ISBN 0-673-38324-5

Scott, Foresman professional books are available for bulk sales at quantity discounts. For information, please contact Marketing Manager, Professional Books Group, Scott, Foresman and Company, 1900 East Lake Avenue, Glenview, IL 60025.

ACKNOWLEDGMENTS

Many people have helped and encouraged me during the writing of this book. I would specifically like to acknowledge the high levels of support afforded me by Richard Patrick of IBM Corporation, Marty Taucher of Microsoft Corporation, and Jeff Segers and Melody Williams of Tandon Corporation.

In addition, I would like to thank Lance Leventhal and Lowell Denning for their helpful suggestions, Frank Damato, Douglas Bryant, and Chinon America for photography, and Joyce Taylor for proofreading.

Finally, I want to thank my wife Joyce and my children Jenny, Valerie, Melody, Neil, Robert, and James for their understanding and support while I was writing this book.

Contents

Introduction

OS/2 is the powerful new multitasking operating system for IBM AT and compatible computers and for the IBM Personal System/2 computers. It runs on systems that use either the 80286 or the 80386 microprocessor.

WHY OS/2 IS IMPORTANT

The majority of personal computers being purchased for business use today, as well as the large installed base of AT class machines, are all potential hosts for the OS/2 operating system. In addition to IBM, computer manufacturers such as Compaq, Zenith, AST, and many more are offering OS/2 with their systems.

OS/2 will be the primary personal computer operating system well into the mid-1990s. A basic understanding of its features and capabilities is essential to anyone who uses IBM-compatible computers.

Application programs that take advantage of the large virtual address space offered by OS/2 (1 gigabyte) are able to perform tasks that would be impossible in a DOS environment, even with extended or expanded memory. In addition, the ability to run several tasks simultaneously using OS/2's multitasking facility speeds up overall productivity in most business settings.

HOW TO USE OS/2

Those people who are already familiar with the single-tasking PC-DOS/MS-DOS operating environment will feel right at home with OS/2 since many of the commands and features of DOS have been carried over to the new system. However, a number of familiar commands have been given expanded capabilities. Furthermore, entirely new features which deal specifically with multitasking must be mastered to get maximum benefit from OS/2.

This book puts all the knowledge needed to use OS/2 successfully into one place. Numerous examples of command usage are included, along with coverage of common mistakes and exercises for the reader. Both new users who are not experienced in using DOS and veterans who have been using DOS for years will find *Guide to*

OS/2 to be a handy reference as well as a thorough introduction to OS/2.

WHO SHOULD USE THIS BOOK?

If you have an AT class computer or an IBM PS/2 Model 50, Model 60, or Model 80, you need this book. OS/2 has been designed to optimize the performance of these machines and to take advantage of their capabilities in a way that DOS can never achieve. To get the most from the investment you have made in your hardware, you should be using OS/2. This book will tell you why and how.

If you are considering purchasing a personal computer system, it is essential that you fully understand the major options available. By any standard, systems that support OS/2 deserve careful consideration. This book will help you to make an informed decision about the capabilities of OS/2. Quite possibly an OS/2-based system will meet your needs better than other available alternatives.

If you are currently working with a DOS-based system, you should know the facts about OS/2. Even if your current DOS-based applications are meeting your needs now, you need to know what possibilities would be opened up to you by OS/2. Most or all of your current DOS applications will run without modification under OS/2. You need not sacrifice any of the investment you have made in DOS-based software when you convert to OS/2.

WHAT IS IN THIS BOOK?

Chapter 1, *Overview*, provides a brief look at the history of microcomputer operating systems, showing how OS/2 is related to the software that preceded it. The various versions and editions of OS/2 are described, and the differences between them are explained.

Chapter 2, *Getting Started*, describes the major hardware components of the systems that run OS/2. It goes on to describe how to install OS/2, how to add application programs to the Program Selector, and how to run them.

Chapter 3, *How OS/2 Works*, explains how features of the 80286 microprocessor chip provide for multitasking and virtual memory. OS/2 takes full advantage of these features. The detailed description of how OS/2 provides virtual memory and multitasking will give you insight into the primary concerns of those who write OS/2 application programs.

Chapter 4, *Using Floppy Disks*, describes the principal device for transferring software from one OS/2 computer to another. Specific attention is given to the commands used to make such information transfers.

Chapter 5, *Using Hard Disks*, deals with the primary on-line storage medium for OS/2 computers. Special emphasis is given to the preparation of a hard disk for use with OS/2 and to the commands used to create a logical data structure on the hard disk.

Chapter 6, *Creating, Copying, and Deleting Files*, describes how OS/2 implements these important file-handling operations. Detailed descriptions of the commands involved, as well as examples, tips, and shortcuts, provide the knowledge needed to maintain an OS/2-based system.

Chapter 7, *Operating on Files*, covers redirection, filters, and pipes, which manipulate files in various ways, and introduces the OS/2 mode grouping symbols.

Chapter 8, *Configuring an OS/2 System*, gives a detailed description of each command that may appear in the system configuration file. OS/2 can be customized to a great extent by the entries in this file.

Chapter 9, *Batch Processing*, describes the powerful OS/2 batch processing facility. This facility allows OS/2 commands and batch subcommands to be combined into programs. Even nonprogrammers can make good use of batch processing.

Chapter 10, *Hard Disk Backup*, describes the options available for hard disk backup and provides specific suggestions on the best ways to assure that important data is safeguarded.

Chapter 11, *Printing*, describes the provision OS/2 has made for producing printed output and describes the spooler, which is needed to keep concurrently running applications from interfering with each other's output to the printer.

Chapter 12, *Command Reference*, gives a thorough description of every OS/2 command, complete with examples of typical usage.

Chapter 1

Overview

INTRODUCTION

WHAT IS OPERATING SYSTEM/2?

THE HISTORICAL BACKGROUND OF OS/2
    Mainframe Evolution
    Microcomputer Evolution

HOW DOES OS/2 RELATE TO THE IBM PS/2 FAMILY OF COMPUTERS?

THE PHASED RELEASE OF OS/2

OS/2 STANDARD EDITION VERSION 1.0

OS/2 STANDARD EDITION VERSION 1.1

OS/2 EXTENDED EDITION VERSION 1.0

OS/2 EXTENDED EDITION VERSION 1.1

HOW IS OS/2 SIMILAR TO DOS? HOW ARE THEY DISSIMILAR?

DOS MODE VS. OS/2 MODE

WHAT DOES OS/2 RUN ON?

SUMMARY

INTRODUCTION

In this chapter, we give a brief overview of OS/2 and what it will do for you. We cover the usage of OS/2, its major components, and how it relates to the most commonly used computer hardware and software. We discuss who stands to gain the most from using OS/2 and why.

WHAT IS OPERATING SYSTEM/2?

Operating System/2 (OS/2) is a single-user, multitasking, virtual memory operating system designed for computers based on the Intel 80286 and 80386 microprocessors. Multitasking means that you will be able to run several application programs at the same time. Virtual memory means that you can run programs even if they require more memory than is physically present in your computer. Marketed by both its developer, Microsoft Corporation, and by IBM Corporation, OS/2 bears a strong resemblance to its predecessor, PC-DOS/MS-DOS. (Hereafter we will refer to PC-DOS and MS-DOS jointly as DOS.) The IBM version of OS/2 is called IBM OS/2, while the Microsoft version is called MS OS/2. They are functionally almost identical, so from now on we will refer to both jointly as OS/2. Just as DOS has been the operating system of choice for the IBM PC and XT, OS/2 is destined to become the primary operating system for IBM AT class machines and the more powerful members of the IBM PS/2 family. An interesting point is that Microsoft does not sell its version of OS/2 to the general public. It sells only to computer manufacturers. The manufacturers, in turn, customize their versions of OS/2 and resell them to their customers.

OS/2 takes much greater advantage of the capabilities of the 286 and 386 processors than DOS was ever able to take. Since OS/2 is not downward compatible with the 8088 processor used in PCs and XTs, it can make use of features found only at and above the 286 level. One of these features is the ability to address 16Mb of memory directly. Another is a powerful and efficient multitasking system. Virtual memory makes it possible to load and execute applications that consume up to a full 16Mb of address space even if the amount of physical memory installed is much smaller. This is accomplished by *swapping* program and data segments that are not currently active out to your hard disk. When they are needed again, OS/2 swaps them back in. At any given moment in time, physical memory (RAM) contains the program code and data that is currently being used. The rest of the code and data for the active tasks is in *virtual* memory, which is a special dedicated area on the hard disk.

THE HISTORICAL BACKGROUND OF OS/2

To gain an understanding of the origins of OS/2, we must return to the beginning of electronic computers themselves. These early machines, which evolved into the large computers that are today called *mainframes*, were the testing ground for many of the important ideas that are incorporated into OS/2. The personal computers that are so familiar to us today have gone through an evolution that closely parallels the evolution of the mainframes, but they have done so much more quickly.

Mainframe Evolution

The first electronic computers were developed during World War II for military applications. They were very large, very expensive to build, and very expensive to run. Since the binary logic they used was so far removed from ordinary human experience, only a very few computer scientists could operate them. Through the 1950s and 1960s, advances in hardware and software brought down the costs of computers and made them easier to use. One of the key advances was the concept of the *operating system*. An operating system is a software program that provides a buffer or interface between the computer hardware and the programs that people write to do useful work. Before operating systems were available, programmers had to understand how computers worked in great detail. Relatively few people had the necessary expertise, and as a result, computer use was restricted to governments, large corporations, and well endowed universities.

In the 1960s, operating systems that provided simpler user interfaces to the applications programmer started to appear. Details of the hardware were masked by the operating system, making programming an easier job and opening up the field to a larger number of people.

As early operating systems were making programming easier, continuing advances in technology were steadily bringing down the cost of computer memory. Great advances were made in read/write memory, also called *random access memory* (RAM) or *main memory*. Rapid strides were also made in hard disk storage, also known as *on-line storage*. These advances made it possible to give computers much more memory than was previously possible. The availability of large memories made it possible to write operating systems that could run several applications (or tasks) at a time.

A key concept of some of these multitasking operating systems is the idea of virtual memory. In a virtual memory system, the operating system "tells" the application program that there is more memory available than is actually present in the computer. For example, it may appear that 8Mb of memory are available when in fact only 2Mb of main memory have been installed.

Virtual memory works on the assumption that, although an application may need to access a total of 8Mb of program code and data at some time during the course of its execution, it does not need all that memory all the time. The parts of the program that are not currently being used can be swapped safely out to hard disk, a slower and much less expensive form of memory. When these "stored" parts of the application are needed, they can be swapped back into main memory with a minimum of delay and be utilized immediately. Thus, virtual memory allows a computer to handle much larger applications than would otherwise be possible. Alternatively, it allows a multitasking operating system to run a large number of jobs simultaneously. Without virtual memory, only a few very small applications could be operated concurrently, making multitasking of dubious value. Virtual memory is the key technology that makes nontrivial multitasking possible.

Microcomputer Evolution

The appearance of 8-bit microprocessor chips (like the Intel 8080 and the MOS Technology 6502) on the market in late 1974 and early 1975 allowed the construction of small desktop computers that rivaled the early mainframes in power. These machines were inexpensive enough that a sufficiently interested individual could actually own his or her own computer. At first, there was very little software and no operating systems available. But soon operating systems began to appear. They were rudimentary by mainframe standards, but were sufficient for machines with the limited power of the early microcomputers. They were, of course, single-tasking operating systems, capable of performing only one task at a time. They also had no provision for supporting devices such as hard disks. The most successful of these early operating systems was CP/M-80 from Digital Research, Inc. It was designed to run on computers that used the Intel 8080 microprocessor or Central Processing Unit (CPU) chip and also worked on systems based on the Zilog Z-80 chip.

When the IBM PC was introduced, it was based on an advanced derivative of the 8080 microprocessor called the 8088. A new operating system was needed since the operating system is more sensitive to hardware changes than any other kind of software because it controls the hardware at the most primitive level. When the new IBM PC was introduced, three operating systems were available for it.

One was CP/M-86, a descendant of the CP/M-80 that had so thoroughly dominated the microcomputer world before the IBM PC arrived. The second was the UCSD p-system, which was quickly *ported* from the 8080 to support the 8088 chip. The p-system, developed at the University of California at San Diego, was very popular at many universities across the United States but had little following in business circles.

The third operating system, which was eventually endorsed by IBM, was Microsoft's MS-DOS. IBM licensed a version of MS-DOS from Microsoft, calling it PC-DOS. Since all the manufacturers of IBM-compatible personal computers wanted to model their products closely to IBM's, they all licensed MS-DOS also. As a result, DOS rose to almost total domination of the operating system market, while CP/M-86 and UCSD p-system faded into obscurity.

The early IBM PCs had a relatively small amount of memory, and the Intel 8088 is a CPU chip of modest power. Furthermore, when the PC was introduced, there was no provision for connecting a hard disk to it, and the largest amount of on-line storage available was a pair of 160Kb floppy disk drives. Thus the hardware was not capable of supporting anything more than a single-tasking operating system. Even at that, the PC could accommodate only small programs. As time went on, IBM introduced upgrades that featured more main memory and higher capacity floppy disks.

More advanced models were placed on the market, including the PC-XT, which included a hard disk, and the PC-AT, which utilized the more advanced Intel 80286 CPU chip. The 286 in the AT could directly address far more memory than the 8088 could. The maximum for the 8088 is 640Kb, while the 80286 can address up to 16Mb. As the clock speeds of 286-based computers rose above 6 MHz and as the cost of RAM chips and hard disks continued to decline, readily available and relatively inexpensive personal computers are now capable of supporting true multitasking. Thus the time is ripe for a multitasking operating system that will run on the 286 and the more advanced 386 chips, and that will make use of virtual memory architecture. OS/2 from Microsoft is such an operating system. Like its predecessor, MS-DOS, a version of OS/2 has been licensed by IBM. As a result, OS/2 is certain to become the single-user multitasking operating system of choice for 286- and 386-based computers used in general business applications. Everyone who uses such computers should become familiar with OS/2.

HOW DOES OS/2 RELATE TO THE IBM PS/2 FAMILY OF COMPUTERS?

The OS/2 operating system and the PS/2 family of personal computers were announced by IBM at the same time. IBM intends that OS/2 be the primary operating system for the PS/2 models that incorporate either a 286 or 386 CPU chip. However, OS/2 is by no means restricted to the PS/2. It will run on any 286- or 386-based machine that has a compatible system Basic Input/Output Subsystem (BIOS). For example, the popular IBM PC-AT will run OS/2 without any problem. So will many AT clones and compatible systems.

> YOU DO NOT NEED AN IBM PS/2 TO RUN OS/2

THE PHASED RELEASE OF OS/2

OS/2 is being released by Microsoft and IBM in three stages. This strategy allows people to gain many of the benefits of using OS/2 before the full system has been completed. The Standard Edition contains virtually all the features that a person operating a stand-alone computer will need. The Extended Edition, available only from IBM, contains additional features that are valuable to people whose computers are connected to a network or those who wish to exchange data with IBM mainframe computers. This book deals primarily with the Standard Edition of OS/2.

OS/2 STANDARD EDITION VERSION 1.0

The first release, Standard Edition Version 1.0, incorporates the following features:
- Supports up to 16Mb of addressable RAM
- Concurrent processing of multiple applications
- High-level programming interface
- Compatibility with DOS 3.3
- Enhanced ease of use
- National language support

The high-level programming interface means that applications programmers are able to access operating system functions without having to resort to assembly language programming. Many useful functions are available by making direct CALLs from such high-level languages as COBOL, Fortran, C, and BASIC.

Among the available ease-of-use features are comprehensive on-line help information and descriptive written system messages (rather than the cryptic codes often provided by DOS). One restriction on this version is that hard disk partitions may be no larger than 32Mb. This implies that Version 1.0 cannot handle files larger than 32Mb.

OS/2 STANDARD EDITION VERSION 1.1

OS/2 Standard Edition Version 1.1 contains all the features of Version 1.0. It supports disk partitions of up to 314Mb, incorporates a System Editor, and in addition includes the Presentation Manager. The Presentation Manager is a windowing and graphics environment that provides the user with a friendlier user interface while simultaneously allowing compatibility with IBM's Systems Application Architecture (SAA). The SAA is designed to allow information exchange across IBM's entire product line—all the way from personal computers to the largest mainframes.

OS/2 EXTENDED EDITION VERSION 1.0

OS/2 Extended Edition Version 1.0 is available only from IBM. Microsoft was not involved in its development. Like Standard Edition Version 1.0, Extended Edition Version 1.0 is limited to disk partitions no larger than 32Mb. It incorporates all the features of the Standard Edition Version 1.0 and in addition includes the Communications Manager and the Database Manager. The new features of the Extended Edition are valuable primarily to people who wish to connect their personal systems to larger IBM computers and exchange information.

The Communications Manager allows concurrent access to other computers via a variety of connectivities including:
- SDLC
- DFT
- IBM Token-Ring Network
- Asynchronous

Multiple protocols can also be used concurrently, including:
- LU6.2
- IBM 3270 Data Stream
- Asynchronous

Multiple terminal types can be concurrently emulated, for example:
- IBM 3270
- IBM 3101
- DEC VT100

In addition, file transfer under terminal emulation is supported, system management information is maintained, and programming interfaces are provided for the various supported connectivities.

The Database Manager supports the IBM relational database model and uses Structured Query Language (SQL). It is consistent with the family of IBM relational database products running on larger computers and can exchange data with them.

OS/2 EXTENDED EDITION VERSION 1.1

OS/2 Extended Edition Version 1.1 contains all the features of Extended Edition Version 1.0. In addition, it supports hard disk partitions of up to 314Mb, incorporates the Presentation Manager, and supports local area networking. It supports IBM's Token-Ring and PC networks and the OS/2 LAN Server, and it provides programming interfaces for IBM NetBIOS and LAN IEEE 802.2. Table 1.1 shows the various editions and versions of OS/2 and the features that each contains.

Table 1.1
Features of the OS/2
Editions and Versions

	Multitasking	Virtual Memory	Maximum Partition Size	Maximum Installed RAM	Database Manager	Communications Manager	Presentation Manager	Local Area Network	System Editor
Standard Edition Version 1.0	Yes	Yes	32Mb	16Mb	No	No	No	No	No
Extended Edition Version 1.0 (IBM only)	Yes	Yes	32Mb	16Mb	Yes	Yes	No	No	No
Standard Edition Version 1.1	Yes	Yes	314Mb	16Mb	No	No	Yes	No	Yes
Extended Edition Version 1.1 (IBM only)	Yes	Yes	314Mb	16Mb	Yes	Yes	Yes	Yes	Yes

HOW IS OS/2 SIMILAR TO DOS? HOW ARE THEY DISSIMILAR?

In most respects OS/2 is very like DOS. A person who is familiar with using DOS will find that most of the DOS commands and conventions work in the same manner under OS/2. Furthermore, thanks to IBM's automatic installation procedure, a standard OS/2 installation is even easier to perform than a standard DOS installation. However, the virtual memory and multitasking features of OS/2 make programming far more complex than it is with DOS.

DOS MODE VS. OS/2 MODE

Since DOS is a single-tasking operating system, programmers who developed applications to run under DOS were justified in assuming that when their program was running, it had complete control of the entire system. Consequently, they often performed operations (such as writing directly to the video screen) that would cause conflicts with other applications if they were to be run in a multitasking environment.

Clearly, users who have a library of DOS applications will want to be able to continue to run them after converting to OS/2. OS/2 makes this possible by offering the option of running DOS applications in DOS (real) mode. DOS mode is a single-tasking operating mode of OS/2. With it, only one DOS mode task can be executed at a time.

OS/2 (protected) mode is the multitasking operating mode of OS/2. Applications written to run under OS/2 mode must adhere to a strict set of rules that assure that concurrently executing applications will not interfere with each other. Thus, any applications running in this mode are "protected" from interference by other applications. As time goes on and more and more protected OS/2 mode applications become available, the need to continue to run DOS mode applications will decrease.

For the *user*, running an OS/2 mode application program is not substantially different from running a DOS application. The external appearance of the programs, also known as the operator interface, can be as similar as desired. However, the situation is quite different for the *applications programmer* who writes OS/2 mode applications. Because of the restrictions dictated by multitasking and the new commands that enforce those restrictions, it is a great deal more difficult to write programs that run properly under OS/2 than it is to write similar programs that run under DOS. OS/2 applications programming requires a higher skill level than does DOS applications programming. In addition, it will take longer to develop a typical OS/2 application than it would take the same programmer to develop a similar DOS program.

WHAT DOES OS/2 RUN ON?

OS/2 will run on any 80286- or 80386-based microcomputer whose manufacturer has assured that the computer's Basic Input/Output Subsystem (BIOS) is compatible with OS/2.

All of the major manufacturers of such machines, i.e. IBM, Compaq, and Zenith, have already announced compatibility. In addition, a host of lesser known manufacturers also produce OS/2-compatible machines. If you have any question as to whether a computer you are about to buy supports OS/2, ask the salesperson to demonstrate OS/2-compatibility before you buy. If you already own a 286 or 386 computer that is not OS/2-compatible, contact the manufacturer to see if an upgrade kit is available. If not, a systems consultant may still be able to get you up and running by giving you a new system BIOS ROM. Just about any 286- or 386-based computer that contains sufficient memory (at least 1.5Mb is recommended) can be made to run OS/2.

SUMMARY

OS/2 is the first single-user, multitasking operating system that is likely to gain such widespread acceptance that it will be installed on millions of computers. It traces its roots back to both multitasking mainframe operating systems and to the single-tasking DOS that is currently installed on millions of IBM and compatible PCs. It offers downward compatibility to existing DOS applications through the DOS mode of operation as well as true multitasking with the OS/2 mode.

It is just about as easy to use programs that have been written to function under OS/2 as it is to use similar DOS programs. However, it is considerably more difficult to *write* OS/2 programs than it is to write similar DOS programs.

OS/2 runs only on computers that incorporate either an 80286 or an 80386 CPU chip. Owners of IBM PCs, XTs, or their compatibles (which all use 8088, 8086, or compatible CPU chips) will have to upgrade to either a 286- or 386-based machine to run OS/2.

Chapter 2

Getting Started

THE COMPUTER
 Memory
 The Video Display
 The Keyboard
 The Floppy Disk Drive
 The Hard Disk Drive

INSTALLING OS/2
 Partitioning the Hard Disk
 Installing an Application

RUNNING AN OS/2 APPLICATION
 Invoking the Session Manager
 Adding Applications to the Session Manager Menu
 Starting Sessions
 Switching between Sessions
 Ending Sessions

SUMMARY

THE COMPUTER

OS/2 is an operating system designed to run on computers based on the Intel 80286 microprocessor. Since the 32-bit Intel 80386 microprocessor incorporates the functions of the 80286 as a subset, OS/2 will also run on 386-based machines. Although any 286- or 386-based machine with sufficient memory is potentially capable of supporting OS/2, the Basic Input/Output System (BIOS) which controls the computer's major input/output devices must be compatible with OS/2. If you wish to run OS/2 on a given brand of 286 or 386 computer, be sure the manufacturer guarantees it to be OS/2-compatible.

It is possible to run OS/2 on an 8088-based PC. If you insert an add-on processor card that contains an 80286 CPU, you will have the functional equivalent of an IBM PC-AT. Performance may be somewhat less than that of an AT, but you will be spared the expense of buying an entirely new machine.

Memory

OS/2 is a major software system that takes up many megabytes of storage. Fortunately, not all of the system is needed all the time. Even so, it is quite possible that OS/2 will need considerably more than a megabyte of system memory to perform some of its functions. Systems hosting the OS/2 operating system in OS/2 mode only must be equipped with at least 1.5 Mb of memory. To run both OS/2 mode and DOS mode, at least 2Mb of memory are needed. OS/2 needs a certain minimum amount of memory to function at all. Above that critical minimum, the performance of OS/2 steadily improves as the amount of memory increases (up to a maximum of 16Mb). This is because OS/2 is designed to take advantage of whatever resources are available to it. The more memory that is available, the more efficient the operation of OS/2 becomes.

Early in the life of OS/2, before a large number of OS/2 mode applications become available, it is critical to have enough memory to support both DOS mode and OS/2 mode.

The Video Display

Although the initial release of OS/2 Standard Edition Version 1.0 does not make use of graphics, Standard Version 1.1 does. Standard Edition Version 1.1 incorporates a graphics-based user interface called Presentation Manager. Presentation Manager bears a strong family resemblance to Microsoft Windows and makes full use of the high-resolution graphics capabilities of the VGA video system in the IBM Personal System/2 machines. OS/2 Extended Edition Version 1.1 has the same video characteristics as Standard Edition Version 1.1.

Version 1.0 of both Editions of OS/2 will run in systems equipped with any of the common video display systems. As well as VGA-equipped systems, it will also work in systems equipped with IBM EGA or CGA systems. The popular Hercules video adapter will also work well with OS/2.

The Keyboard

There are two different keyboard layouts that will be found on computers that run OS/2. The first is the standard IBM PC-AT keyboard and its compatibles. Figure 2.1 shows the AT keyboard.

Figure 2.1
The IBM PC-AT Keyboard

The second layout is that of the IBM PS/2 keyboard and its compatibles. Figure 2.2 depicts the PS/2 keyboard. As you can see, they contain most of the same keys. Only the placement of some of the keys is different.

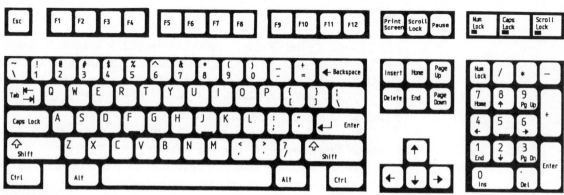

Figure 2.2
The IBM PS/2 Keyboard

**The Floppy
Disk Drive**

Unless it is a node on a network or it incorporates a removable hard disk, your computer is certain to have at least one floppy disk drive. Floppy disks provide the primary method of transporting software and data from one computer to another. They may also be used to duplicate or *back up* information contained on your system's hard disk drive.

There are several different types of floppy disk drives that might be attached to a system running OS/2. We will briefly describe each of them.

The first type of floppy disk drive is called a 360K drive. It uses diskettes that are 5.25 inches square and have a capacity of 360,000 bytes. These diskettes are commonly called double-sided double-density (DSDD) diskettes because they store information on both sides of the diskette platter, and the information is packed twice as densely as it was on the original 5.25-inch floppy disks. This type of diskette is common on IBM PC and XT machines and their compatibles as well as on the AT class machines that run OS/2. More computers currently use 360K floppies than all other floppy types combined.

The second type of floppy disk drive, called the 1.2Mb floppy, also uses a diskette that is 5.25 inches square, but holds 1,200,000 bytes (1.2Mb) of data. It is called a high density (HD) diskette, and stores data even more densely than the DSDD diskette does. In external appearance, however, both the drive and the diskette look identical to the DSDD drive and diskette. First introduced on the IBM PC-AT, this drive is also found on AT-compatibles and 386-based machines. Many computers contain both a 1.2Mb and a 360K floppy drive. The 360K floppy is largely used to handle data that is exchanged with PC and XT class machines (which do not support the 1.2Mb device).

The third type of floppy disk drive, which is standard on 286- and 386-based IBM PS/2 machines, has a 1.44Mb capacity. The 1.44Mb diskette is 3.5 inches square and looks quite different from the 5.25-inch diskettes mentioned earlier. Figure 2.3 shows typical 1.2Mb, 360Kb, and 1.44Mb diskette drives.

IBM switched from 5.25-inch to 3.5-inch disk drives as a part of a general downsizing of their personal computer products. Many aspects of the Personal System/2 machines have been miniaturized. As a result, PS/2 machines take up less desk space than AT machines of comparable power.

Since OS/2 runs equally well on machines having 5.25- or 3.5-inch diameter diskettes, it may make sense to equip your machine with at least one floppy drive of each size. In that way you can be sure that you will be able to use any software and data that has been developed for OS/2 regardless of the system on which it was generated.

You may rightly ask, "How can I install a big, bulky 5.25-inch floppy disk drive into the downsized PS/2 models? The expansion space provided is only large enough to hold a 3.5-inch drive." The answer is simple enough. External floppy disk subsystems are available that connect to the PS/2 computers via cable. IBM has such a subsystem, as do several third party subsystem vendors, such as Dolphin Systems Technology of Santa Ana, California. Figure 2.4 shows the Dolphin Matchmaker™, a 5.25-inch external floppy disk subsystem for PS/2.

It is good to know that there are also 3.5-inch floppy disk drives in the market that have a capacity of 720,000 bytes. For instance, the IBM Personal System/2 Models 25 and 30 incorporate such drives. However, neither of these machines will run OS/2. It is unlikely that you will have any need for a 720K drive on your OS/2 system. If you do have a use for such a drive, you can install an IBM 720K drive directly into the 286- and 386-based AT-compatible machines. OS/2 is compatible with the 720K drives.

The Hard Disk Drive

As we mentioned earlier, the complete OS/2 operating system takes up several megabytes of storage. In addition, typical application software is likely to consume even more storage space. It is clear that

(PHOTO COURTESY OF CHINON AMERICA INC.)

**Figure 2.3
1.2Mb, 360Kb, and
1.44Mb Diskette Drives**

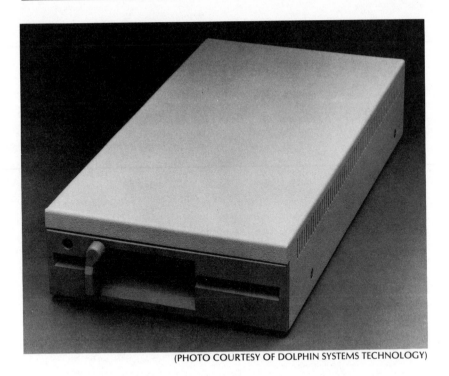

(PHOTO COURTESY OF DOLPHIN SYSTEMS TECHNOLOGY)

**Figure 2.4
Dolphin Matchmaker,
External 5.25-inch
Floppy Subsystem**

it would be impractical to operate OS/2 on a computer that has only floppy disk drives as on-line storage devices.

The most practical on-line storage device for OS/2 systems is a hard disk drive. Hard disks come in capacities ranging from 20Mb up to several hundred megabytes. At least one such drive must be present on any system running OS/2. To assure the best possible performance, procure a hard disk that has the fastest access time and transfer rate that you can afford. Also make sure that its capacity is large enough to meet your needs. A 20Mb hard disk is just about big enough to hold all of OS/2 Extended Edition, with very little room left over for applications software. You should probably have at least 40Mb of hard disk storage on line. For some applications, you will need much more. Think carefully about your current and future needs before buying a hard disk that you will soon outgrow. Figure 2.5 shows 60Mb and 120Mb third-party hard disk subsystems for the IBM PS/2 Model 60, or PC-AT.

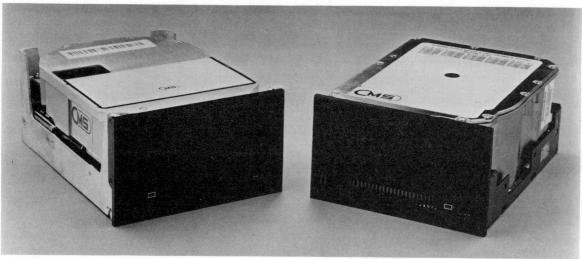

(PHOTO COURTESY OF CMS ENHANCEMENTS, INC.)

**Figure 2.5
60Mb and 120Mb
Hard Disk Subsystems**

INSTALLING OS/2

Installing OS/2 on your computer is fairly easy since automatic installation programs are provided. However, there are pitfalls that may trap the uninitiated. The first prerequisite to a successful installation is proper hardware configuration. You must have all the required hardware, and it must be properly installed. Be sure your system meets the following minimum requirements.

1. Computer: 286- or 386-based processor with OS/2 compatible BIOS.
2. Memory: At least 1.5Mb for Standard Edition 1.0, 2.0Mb for Standard Edition 1.1, 3.0Mb for Extended Edition. Some applications may require more.
3. Floppy Disk: At least one high capacity drive (either a 1.2Mb 5.25-inch drive or a 1.44Mb 3.5-inch drive).
4. Hard Disk: At least one hard disk drive with a capacity of at least 20Mb.
5. Video: CGA, EGA, VGA, Hercules or equivalent graphics adapter and monitor combination.

In addition to the proper hardware, you will also need the diskettes that come with OS/2. The Installation Diskette contains the OS/2 installation program, while the other diskettes hold the OS/2 program files.

Partitioning the Hard Disk

If your hard disk is already set up for IBM PC-DOS or MS-DOS, you may not have to repartition it with OS/2. Since the OS/2 file structure is the same as the DOS file structure and since the OS/2 system files are smaller than the DOS system files, you can copy OS/2 directly onto your hard disk.

By invoking the OS/2 automatic installation procedure, you will replace the OS/2 system files and set the system up for OS/2 operation without disturbing your DOS applications. Most DOS applications will run under the DOS mode of OS/2. Possible exceptions are timing-dependent communications programs and graphics programs that write directly to the video screen. To run these programs you will have to use DOS instead of OS/2. You can boot DOS from a floppy disk whenever you want to run a program that is incompatible with OS/2 since the IBM version of OS/2 cannot share a hard disk with a DOS partition.

If your hard disk does not already have a DOS partition that you wish to retain, you must install a new partition for OS/2. This can be done with the FDISK program that you will find on your Program Disk, or with the version of FDISK that came with your DOS. The IBM version of OS/2 is not designed to share a hard disk with a DOS partition, but the Microsoft version does have that capability. Thus, if you obtain your OS/2 from a computer manufacturer other than IBM, you will be able to put both a DOS partition and an OS/2 partition on the same hard disk. If you would like to have both a DOS partition and an OS/2 partition on your hard disk, use the DOS version of FDISK rather than the OS/2 version. This is necessary because PC-DOS versions earlier than DOS 3.3 do not recognize partitions created with OS/2. Compatible computers such as those manufactured by Compaq Computer Corporation should also be partitioned with their own DOS for the same reason.

You may or may not wish to create a DOS partition on your hard disk. If you will never want to run DOS, do not waste disk space by setting aside a partition for it. Since it is possible to run a DOS program in the real mode of OS/2, you may never need to run DOS.

In any case, there is one additional partition that you may want to set aside in addition to your OS/2 partition. You should create a partition for the swapper. In Chapter 1, we mentioned that OS/2 is a virtual memory operating system. Parts of the active programs that are not being used are swapped out to a designated area on disk, where they are held until they are needed. It is best to place this swap area into a partition of its own. If you set aside only an OS/2 partition and do your swapping within it, the swap area will eventually take over all the free space on the disk. Once disk space is used by the swapper, it becomes unavailable for other uses. There is no provision for automatically recovering swap space. It must be recovered manually through a difficult procedure.

The solution is to create a partition for the swapper. This will keep the swap space within predetermined bounds. A good rule of thumb is to set aside about twice as much swap space as you have system memory. So, for instance if you have 2Mb of RAM it would be reasonable to create a 4Mb partition for the swapper. If you are running very large applications, you may want to make the swap partition larger.

Once your disk is partitioned, you must format each partition. Before you perform the format, you must decide whether you want DOS or OS/2 to be your primary operating environment. You will want to boot directly from your hard disk into your primary operating environment. The secondary operating environment can be accessed by booting from floppy.

Case I—There Is No DOS Partition

In this case, when you partition the disk with FDISK, make logical drive "C" the OS/2 partition. Perform the following procedure:

1. Boot your computer with the OS/2 Installation Diskette.
2. Follow the installation instructions on the screen. You will be asked a series of questions about the configuration you want. The automatically generated configuration is one that will work well for most users.
3. Remove the Installation Diskette from the floppy drive and reboot the system. The Program Selector screen will appear (Figure 2.6).

The OS/2 operating system has now been installed on your hard disk and is operational.

Case II—There Is a DOS Partition, and It Is the Primary
Operating Environment (Only Applies to Microsoft OS/2)

In this case, DOS is installed in logical drive "C:" and is the environment entered when the system boots from hard disk. Microsoft nomenclature differs slightly from IBM's and the locations of some files vary also. These differences are reflected in the instructions below. Format the hard disk in accordance with the instructions

```
Update                                            |  F1=Help

                         Program Selector

   To select a program, press ←, →, ↑, or ↓.   Then, press Enter.
          To select Update, press F10.   Then, Press Enter.

┌─────────────────────────────┐   ┌─────────────────────────────┐
│                             │   │                             │
│   Start a Program           │   │   Switch to a Running Program│
│   ───────────────           │   │   ──────────────────────────│
│                             │   │                             │
│ • Introducing OS/2          │   │ • DOS Command Prompt        │
│ • OS/2 Command Prompt       │   │                             │
│                             │   │                             │
│                             │   │                             │
│                             │   │                             │
│                             │   │                             │
│                             │   │                             │
│                             │   │                             │
│                             │   │                             │
└─────────────────────────────┘   └─────────────────────────────┘
```

Figure 2.6
OS/2 Program
Selector Screen

in your MS-DOS manual. Assuming you partitioned your hard disk so that the OS/2 partition was designated drive "D:", perform the following procedure:

1. Make a copy of your MS-OS/2 PROGRAM diskette and put the original in a safe place.
2. Boot your system off your new copy of the PROGRAM diskette.
3. Format the OS/2 partition with the following command:
   FORMAT D:
4. Install the system files on the hard disk by typing:
   INSTFLP
5. Reboot the machine. Since the computer is booting from floppy, the [A:\] prompt will appear.
6. Remove the PROGRAM diskette from the floppy drive and insert the SUPPLEMENTAL diskette. Enter:
   COPY A:*.* C:\os2

Important note: In systems booted from floppy disk, the device drivers are not kept in the root directory as is normally the case. Instead they are kept in a subdirectory named "\OS2SYS". Thus, device statements in the configuration file should be altered to show the new location of the drivers. For example, the statement

```
DEVICE=D:\mouse.....
```

should be changed to

```
DEVICE=D:\OS2SYS\mouse.....
```

Configuration files will be covered in detail in Chapter 8.

Installing an Application

Once OS/2 has been installed and is running, you may copy application programs into your OS/2 partition. You may also copy in language assemblers, compilers, and interpreters that will allow you to write your own applications. Most applications will have an installation program that will copy the application to your OS/2 hard disk partition and configure it to run on your system. If you are copying files yourself, refer to the discussion of the COPY command in Chapter 4 of this book.

RUNNING AN OS/2 APPLICATION

Once OS/2 and your application programs have been installed, you are ready to do some real work. When you power up your system or reboot by simultaneously depressing the Ctrl, Alt, and Del keys, OS/2 will take control, switch to protected mode operation, and display the Program Selector Screen shown in Figure 2.6. This screen is also known as the Session Manager Screen, since it is the visible portion of the Session Manager, which controls the running of all the applications that are executing at any one time.

Invoking the Session Manager

The Session Manager oversees the beginning and terminating of applications as well as switching the foreground task from one application to another. Once OS/2 is running, you can bring the main Session Manager Menu onto the screen at any time by simultaneously depressing Ctrl and Esc.

There are two boxes on the Session Manager Screen, one labeled "Start a Program," the other labeled "Switch to a Running Program." Since you are using the Session Manager for the first time, there are no programs listed in either box. In the "Switch to a Running Program" box on the right there is one entry, "DOS Command Prompt." If you select "DOS Command Prompt," you will enter DOS mode and find yourself at the DOS mode command prompt. In the "Start a Program" box there are two entries, "Introducing OS/2" and "OS/2 Command Prompt." "Introducing OS/2" is a brief entry-level tutorial. If you press the Enter key while the "OS/2 Command Prompt" option is highlighted, you will be sent to the OS/2 mode command prompt. To return to the Session Manager, just press Ctrl-Esc again.

When you are back at the Session Manager Screen, you will notice that a change has taken place. There is a new entry in the "Switch to a Running Program" box. It is "OS/2 Command Prompt" (see Figure 2.7). When you selected the "OS/2 Command Prompt" option from the "Start a Program" menu, OS/2 actually started a session. Now there is an OS/2 mode session and a DOS mode session available for use. However, not much is happening in the new OS/2 mode session right now. The command prompt is waiting for a command to be entered from the keyboard.

```
Update                                                        |  F1=Help

                          Program Selector

       To select a program, press ←, →, ↑, or ↓.  Then, press Enter.
          To select Update, press F10.  Then, press Enter.

 ┌─────────────────────────────┐    ┌─────────────────────────────┐
 │   Start a Program           │    │  Switch to a Running Program │
 │   ───────────────           │    │  ─────────────────────────── │
 │                             │    │                              │
 │ ▪ Introducing OS/2          │    ┊ ▪ DOS Command Prompt         │
 │ ▪ OS/2 Command Prompt       │    │ ▪ OS/2 Command Prompt        │
 │                             │    │                              │
 │                             │    │                              │
 │                             │    │                              │
 │                             │    │                              │
 │                             │    │                              │
 │                             │    │                              │
 │                             │    │                              │
 └─────────────────────────────┘    └─────────────────────────────┘
```

Figure 2.7
Session Manager Screen
after an OS/2 Mode
Session Has Been Started

*Adding Applications
to the Session
Manager Menu*

After you have installed several application programs, you will probably want to execute them. In order for OS/2 to run these programs concurrently, the Session Manager must be made aware of them. To demonstrate how this works, let's write a couple of very trivial applications and add them to the Session Manager list of programs. First, let's create a "scratch" directory to hold these test files. It is a good idea to keep the root directory as free of nonessential files as possible. Move the highlighted cursor to the "Switch to a Running Program" box and select the "OS/2 Command Prompt" option by pressing the Enter key. At the command prompt, enter the following commands:

```
MKDIR \scratch
CHDIR \scratch
```

These two commands create a new subdirectory named "scratch," then make "scratch" the current directory. The creation of subdirectories is treated in detail in Chapter 5. We can create a very simple program as follows:

```
COPY con prog1.cmd/a
:START
ECHO Program 1 is running.
GOTO START
^Z
```

In Chapter 6 we will elaborate on the creation of small command files with the COPY command. For now, let's just enter this program into the computer. It creates a program named "prog1.cmd." All the program does is display a message on the screen, proclaiming "Program 1 is running." Then it loops back to the :START label and does it again. The program is an infinite loop. It will continue running and continue displaying its message until execution is aborted by depressing Ctrl-C at the keyboard. The "^Z" character on the last line is created by depressing Ctrl-Z. All command (or batch) files created with the COPY command must be terminated with the Ctrl-Z character.

To show multitasking, we must have at least two programs executing concurrently, so let's create another one.

```
COPY con prog2.cmd/a
:START
ECHO Program 2 is running.
GOTO START
^Z
```

We now have two programs that can be run concurrently and that will give visual evidence on the screen that they are running. Now return to the Session Manager by depressing Ctrl-Esc.

We can add programs to our Session Manager list with the "Update" function mentioned at the top of the Session Manager Screen. When you press function key F10, a window appears in the upper left hand corner of the screen, containing the Update Menu. After you press Enter, a highlight bar appears on the first option on the menu. Figure 2.8 shows the Update menu.

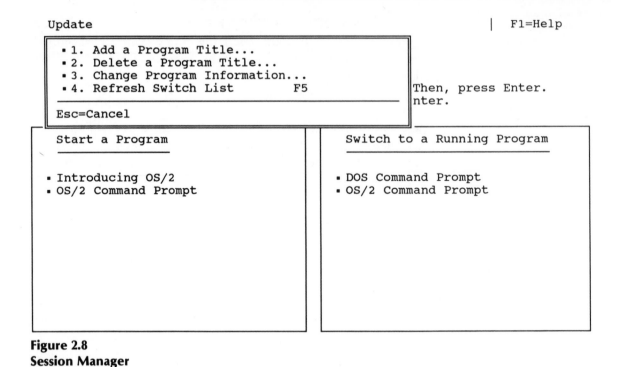

Figure 2.8
Session Manager
Update Menu

There are four options on the Update Menu. The one that concerns us now is the first one, "Add a Program Title. . . ." Press Enter to highlight the desired option, then Enter again to select it. Now a new window appears, named "Add a Program Title." The screen is as shown in Figure 2.9.

With "Program Title" highlighted, enter "First Test Program." Then use the down arrow key to move the highlight bar to "Program Pathname." If you press the Enter key after you have typed in the program title, the Session Manager will assume that you are completely through with the add operation and will not allow you to enter path information. You must use the down arrow to move the highlighted bar down. With "Program Pathname" highlighted, enter "C:\scratch\prog1.cmd". In this simple example, our program does not have any parameters, so we need not proceed down to the "Program Parameters" option. Press the Enter Key to complete the addition. If any of this sounds confusing or unclear, you can get more explanation from the context-sensitive help that is available. Just

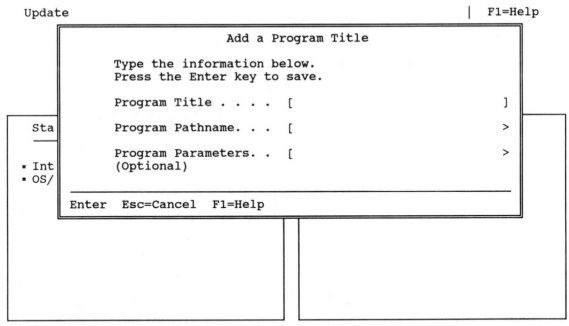

Figure 2.9
Add a Program
Title Window of
Session Manager

press the F1 key to display help text about the function in which you are currently engaged. After you have read the help text, pressing Esc will take you back to where you were before asking for help.

After returning to the Session Manager Screen, press F10 again and repeat the above procedure to add "prog2.cmd." After both programs are added, the Session Manager Screen looks like Figure 2.10.

Starting Sessions

To start your first program, use the arrow keys to move the highlight bar to "First Test Program," then press Enter. A session is created for this program, and execution is started. The message "Program 1 is running." starts to appear repeatedly on the screen and scroll off the top. Press Ctrl-Esc to return to the Session Manager.

Now select "Second Test Program" from the "Start a Program" box. The second application will begin running and displaying

```
Update                                          |   F1=Help

                        Program Selector

   To select a program, press ←, →, ↑, or ↓.  Then, press Enter.
         To select Update, press F10.  Then, press Enter.

 ┌──────────────────────────────┐    ┌──────────────────────────────┐
 │  Start a Program             │    │  Switch to a Running Program │
 │  ─────────────────           │    │  ──────────────────────────  │
 │                              │    │                              │
 │  • First Test Program        │    │  • DOS Command Prompt        │
 │  • Introducing OS/2          │    │  • OS/2 Command Prompt       │
 │  • OS/2 Command Prompt       │    │                              │
 │  • Second Test Program       │    │                              │
 │                              │    │                              │
 │                              │    │                              │
 │                              │    │                              │
 │                              │    │                              │
 │                              │    │                              │
 └──────────────────────────────┘    └──────────────────────────────┘
```

Figure 2.10
Session Manager
Screen with Two
Programs Added

"Program 2 is running." When you return to the Session Manager Screen, it looks like Figure 2.11.

OS/2 allows you to run multiple copies of the same program at the same time. We can demonstrate this capability by selecting "Second Test Program" again from the "Start a Program" Menu. A third active session is created, displaying the message "Program 2 is running." Returning to the Session Manager Screen, we see that it has been updated to reflect the added activity as shown in Figure 2.12.

Switching between Sessions

There are two ways of switching between sessions. One is obvious. You may always leave the currently active session by pressing Ctrl-Esc. This will take you to the Session Manager, from which you can enter a different session. It is also possible to directly switch from one session to another. If you press Alt-Esc instead of Ctrl-Esc, the Session Manager will switch you directly to the next session. By pressing Alt-Esc several times, you can cycle through all the sessions until you come upon the one you want.

```
Update                                            |  F1=Help

                         Program Selector

      To select a program, press ←, →, ↑, or ↓.  Then, press Enter.
          To select Update, press F10.  Then, press Enter.

  ┌─────────────────────────────┐    ┌──────────────────────────────┐
  │  Start a Program            │    │  Switch to a Running Program │
  │  ─────────────────          │    │  ──────────────────────────  │
  │                             │    │                              │
  │  • First Test Program       │    │  • DOS Command Prompt        │
  │  • Introducing OS/2         │    │  • OS/2 Command Prompt       │
  │  • OS/2 Command Prompt      │    │  • First Test Program        │
  │  • Second Test Program      │    │  • Second Test Program       │
  │                             │    │                              │
  │                             │    │                              │
  │                             │    │                              │
  │                             │    │                              │
  │                             │    │                              │
  └─────────────────────────────┘    └──────────────────────────────┘
```

Figure 2.11
The First and Second
Test Programs Are
Now Running

Ending Sessions

Since your system's resources must be shared among all the sessions that are running, it stands to reason that the fewer sessions that are running, the faster an individual session will run. Terminate unnecessary sessions so the remaining sessions will run better. In order to terminate a session, you must first halt the execution of the application that is running in it. Many applications will allow you to quit by making a menu selection. Others will quit automatically when they have run to completion. Some applications, like our little command files "prog1.cmd" and "prog2.cmd," do not have any provision for stopping. Programs such as these can be halted by pressing Ctrl-C.

Once the execution of the application has ceased within the active session and the command prompt is displayed on the screen, you can terminate the session by typing EXIT at the command prompt. You are returned to the Session Manager. On the screen, the list of running programs is now shorter. The session you exited is no longer listed.

```
Update                                                    |  F1=Help

                          Program Selector
       To select a program, press ←, →, ↑, or ↓.  Then, press Enter.
            To select Update, press F10.  Then, press Enter.

 ┌─────────────────────────────────┐  ┌─────────────────────────────────┐
 │   Start a Program               │  │  Switch to a Running Program     │
 │   ─────────────────             │  │  ──────────────────────────      │
 │                                 │  │                                  │
 │ ▪ First Test Program            │  │ ▪ DOS Command Prompt             │
 │ ▪ Introducing OS/2              │  │ ▪ OS/2 Command Prompt            │
 │ ▪ OS/2 Command Prompt           │  │ ▪ First Test Program             │
 │ ▪ Second Test Program           │  │ ▪ Second Test Program 1          │
 │                                 │  │ ▪ Second Test Program 2          │
 │                                 │  │                                  │
 │                                 │  │                                  │
 │                                 │  │                                  │
 │                                 │  │                                  │
 │                                 │  │                                  │
 │                                 │  │                                  │
 └─────────────────────────────────┘  └─────────────────────────────────┘
```

Figure 2.12
Two Copies of the
Second Test Program
Are Active

SUMMARY

In this chapter we discussed the various components of an 80286- or 80386-based computer system and the steps involved in installing OS/2 on such a system. We then covered the installation of application programs, and the use of the Session Manager to execute multiple applications concurrently. The creation, operation, and deletion of individual sessions was explained. In the next several chapters we will learn what OS/2 is, as well as how it handles floppy disks, hard disks, and the files that reside on those disks. This knowledge will be essential if you are to utilize OS/2 fully.

Chapter 3

How OS/2 Works

THE LIMITATIONS OF DOS

REAL ADDRESS MODE ON THE 8088

THE 286 PROTECTED MODE
  Protected Mode Operation

MEMORY MANAGEMENT _single_
  Storage Overcommitment
  How Can We Get Away with Storage
    Overcommitment?
  How Does OS/2 Know What Needs to Be in RAM
    and What Can Be Safely Swapped out to Disk?
  Segment Swapping
  Segment Discard
  Segment Motion
  Protection

HARDWARE PROTECTION
  Separate Address Spaces
  Controlled Access to I/O
  Privilege Levels
  Protection of Data
  Protection of Code
  Input/Output Instructions
  System Critical Instructions

MULTITASKING
  Task Management
  Sessions, Processes, and Threads
  Processes and Threads
  Data Sharing among Processes
  Choosing a Multitasking Level
  Interprocess Communication

SUMMARY

THE LIMITATIONS OF DOS

To gain a proper perspective on OS/2, we must first look at a little history. DOS has been the primary operating system of IBM Personal Computers and compatibles since the IBM PC was first introduced. What has happened over the last several years to prompt the introduction of an entirely new operating system?

For one thing, the capabilities of personal computer hardware have increased steadily. The cost of memory has dropped dramatically, making very large memories feasible. Processor speeds have more than doubled and are on the verge of doubling again. Hard disk drives have increased in capacity and performance and decreased in cost. Thus the modestly priced personal computers of today boast memory sizes, processor speeds, and quantities of fast on-line storage that were not anticipated by either IBM or Microsoft when they introduced the first IBM PC with DOS 1.0.

Secondly, personal computer software has also made amazing progress. As improvements in hardware have provided faster and more powerful machines, the software producers have been quick to take advantage of these advances by introducing application software with greatly expanded capabilities.

Of course, the operating system that mediates between the hardware and the application software (DOS) has evolved also, and its capabilities have been enhanced in many important ways. However, since DOS is based on the architecture of the 8088 microprocessor that forms the heart of the IBM-PC and its successor, the IBM-XT, it is subject to the basic limitations of that microprocessor chip.

Let's enumerate some major limitations that the 8088 chip places on DOS.

1. It is not possible to directly address more than 640K of memory. Various types of extended and expanded memory have been devised, but they require that the memory be partitioned into segments. They do not allow direct access to large unbroken expanses of memory.

2. There is no hardware provision for memory management. It is difficult to run programs whose size exceeds the amount of memory physically present. The application program must take responsibility for the task of swapping resources in and out of memory as they are needed.

3. There is no hardware provision for multitasking, and there is no protection to prevent one task from disrupting another. There are many occasions when you may wish to execute several applications simultaneously. For example, you may

want to edit a document with your wordprocessor at the same time that your spreadsheet program is making a recalculation of a large spreadsheet. Some software implementations of multitasking have been developed to run under DOS, but they are not very efficient, and it is possible for a software bug in one application to upset the processing of another.

REAL ADDRESS MODE ON THE 8088

The registers in the 8088 chip are 16 bits long. Addresses are maintained in segment registers which, when combined with offsets, form a 20-bit address. Twenty-address bits allow the processor to directly access 1Mb of memory.

Programs executing on the 8088 may access any address in memory and may control any I/O device directly. This means that faulty applications can interfere with the operating system, causing it to *crash* or enter an unknown and unrecoverable state. It is risky to multitask in such an environment. A bug in one application could crash all the others that are running at the same time.

THE 286 PROTECTED MODE

The 80286 microprocessor chip is a more powerful successor to the 8088. It is faster than the 8088 and is able to directly address 16Mb of memory rather than the 1Mb addressed by the 8088. However, the advantages of the 286 go beyond mere speed and addressability. The 286 hardware supports multitasking and memory management.

Protected Mode Operation

The 286 supports two modes of operation, real address mode and protected virtual address mode. In real mode, the 286 acts like an 8088. It operates about four times faster than an 8088, but like the 8088 it is limited to directly addressing 1Mb of memory. In protected virtual address mode, also known as protected mode, 24 address lines are used, giving direct addressability to 16Mb of memory. This memory is not accessed directly, however. The segment registers no longer contain references to actual physical locations. Instead, they refer to locations in a *logical* address space. Each program running on the system has access to a logical address space of 1 gigabyte. With this system, it is possible to run programs that are larger than the amount of memory that is physically present in the computer.

In protected mode, multitasking hardware present in the 286 may also be used. In order to run multiple tasks on a single processor, there must be some mechanism for saving the state of the currently executing task and swapping in the next task to be executed. The 286 contains hardware that handles task state maintenance and task switching. The memory management hardware of the 286 assures that different tasks are kept in separate address spaces, thus preventing one application from damaging the code or data of another application.

The protection available with the 286 comes in layers called *privilege levels*. Applications, which operate at a low privilege level, are not allowed to leave their assigned memory space or directly access I/O devices. They must go through the operating system to make use of any system resource. These restrictions make program debugging much easier, since application bugs will not crash the entire system. The programmer can use debugging tools available with OS/2 to track down problems in program code.

OS/2 itself runs at a higher privilege level than the applications do. This allows the operating system to control the activity of several applications and to provide them with the resources they need. When multiple programs require access to the same data in memory, OS/2 can provide the means for all of them to access it. Such sharing of data is carefully controlled so that no one application can corrupt another by virtue of the fact that they both have access to a common data set.

MEMORY MANAGEMENT

We have talked briefly about the segment registers in the 8088. The registers, when combined with an offset, contain the address of a real location in memory. In the 286 the situation is a little more complex. Rather than containing a memory address, the segment register contains an offset or index into a segment table maintained by OS/2. This table is called a descriptor table. The value in the segment register, called a selector, specifies which descriptor table to use and is an index into that descriptor table. Each entry in the descriptor table, called a descriptor, points to a physical memory address. Figure 3.1 shows the relationship between a segment register, a descriptor table, and physical memory.

The use of descriptor tables allows the 286 to handle multiple tasks. There is a global descriptor table (GDT) that contains addresses of resources common to all tasks that are running. In addition, each task has its own local descriptor table (LDT). At any given instant, only one task is active. The descriptor table associated with that task and the GDT are in use. When the task changes, a new

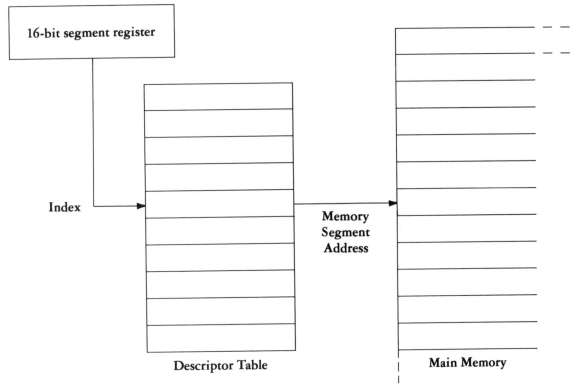

**Figure 3.1
Effective Memory
Address Calculation
in Protected Mode**

LDT will be accessed. Only one GDT, however, is needed to support all the tasks. Figure 3.2 shows how the descriptor tables reference address space.

Each application has its own LDT that defines a private address space for it. No other application may enter the private address space. In addition, the GDT gives access to system-wide data and to programs that are shared among all applications. Together, the LDT and GDT provide access to a 1 gigabyte (1,000Mb) virtual address space. This architecture provides what is called a *virtual memory system*. It is virtual in the sense that applications are able to operate as if there is more memory available than is actually physically present.

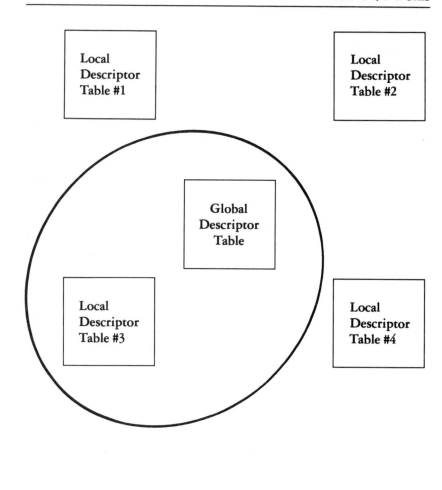

Figure 3.2
Address Space for
Task 3 Is Specified by
the GDT and LDT #3

Storage
Overcommitment

We said earlier that the maximum amount of physical storage that the 286 processor is capable of directly addressing is 16Mb. Many systems will have less than 16Mb of RAM. However, OS/2's memory management system is designed to provide virtual address spaces of up to 1 gigabyte in size. It is highly likely that the memory needs of all tasks running at a particular time will exceed physical memory. In fact, the memory needs of even one single program may exceed physical memory. OS/2 not only allows, but encourages such storage overcommitment.

The ability to run programs which are larger than memory is one of the primary motivations for migrating from DOS to OS/2.

How Can We Get Away with Storage Overcommitment?

You might reasonably ask how we can possibly run one or more programs that require more memory than is physically present in the computer. The answer is that we cannot. We still need as much storage as our programs require. The key point is the *kind* of storage. It is not necessary that all the storage be RAM. Some of it can be hard disk. Hard disk storage is considerably cheaper than RAM on a cost-per-megabyte basis. We can combine RAM and hard disk storage to build our virtual address space.

How Does OS/2 Know What Needs to Be in RAM and What Can Be Safely Swapped out to Disk?

The major premise of the OS/2 memory management system is that not all of the applications' code and data are needed all the time. A determination must be made as to what information is most likely to be needed next. That information should be retained in RAM (or real memory). The rest can be swapped out to disk in a process called *segment swapping*.

Segment Swapping

Based on exhaustive statistical studies of a wide range of applications, it has been found that information that has been used recently is very likely to be used again soon. Conversely, information that has not been used in a long time is unlikely to be used any time soon. Thus, it makes sense to keep those segments that have been used most recently in real memory. Whenever a segment is needed that is not present in RAM, a place must be made for it in RAM. To do this, one of the segments presently residing in RAM must be swapped out. You want to swap out the segment that is least likely to be needed again soon. OS/2 assumes that the segment that is least likely to be needed soon is the segment that was used least recently. It uses a least-recently-used (LRU) algorithm to decide which segment to swap out to disk.

Segment Discard

Sometimes it is possible to recover RAM space without resorting to segment swapping. Segment swapping is required only if the least-recently-used segment has been altered by the processing of the application. If data within the segment has been changed, then the current state of the segment must be preserved in the swap area on disk. However, if the segment to be removed from RAM has not been changed in any way since it was originally loaded in from disk, we do not need to write it to the swap area. We can merely discard it. Later, when that segment is needed again, it can be read in from its original location on disk. By discarding unchanged segments rather than swapping them, we extend the amount of swap area available for other segments. This effectively enlarges the virtual memory space supported by a specific system.

Segment Motion

Since segments are not of a fixed length, after a number of swaps and discards have taken place, *holes* of deallocated memory are sprinkled throughout real memory. This effect, called *fragmentation*, reduces performance, since individual holes may not be large enough to hold the next segment you wish to use, but collectively, if all the holes were to coalesce, there would be enough room. OS/2 has the capability of moving segments to group holes together to satisfy a memory request, thus automatically curing the fragmentation problem.

Protection

Applications are restricted by OS/2 to those segments of memory that have been assigned to them. In this way, all applications are protected from access and possible alteration by other applications running concurrently.

HARDWARE PROTECTION

The 286 provides several mechanisms in the hardware to protect the integrity of the system. These mechanisms are used by OS/2 and relieve the application programmer of worries that other applications might be able to disrupt the execution of his or her application.

Separate Address Spaces

As mentioned above, one protection mechanism is the maintenance of a separate address space for each application. OS/2 makes sure that no application performs an operation that would take execution beyond the bounds of the application's assigned address space. This provision goes a long way toward preventing both intentional and unintentional damage. Intentional damage is possible in a system without strictly separated address spaces. One application programmer may want to destroy the work of another. Unintentional damage is also a real threat. If unproven code contains *bugs* or erroneous statements that cause the program to act in an unforeseen manner, the entire system and all the applications running under it are in jeopardy. The hardware protection built into OS/2 prevents both of these possible sources of damage.

However, other problems are possible, requiring additional protections.

Controlled Access to I/O

In a multitasking environment where several tasks are executing simultaneously, imagine that two or more tasks involve printing something on the printer during the same period of time. If applications had direct access to such devices as the system printer, the result would be unpredictable and almost certainly worthless.

Groups of characters from one job would be intermixed with output from another job, creating an incomprehensible garble. The same problem occurs if two or more programs try to display something on the terminal screen at the same time. On the other hand, if more than one application is waiting for input from the keyboard, some of the operator's keystrokes may go to the intended application, but others may go somewhere else, causing bizarre results in both applications.

To prevent problems of this nature, OS/2 requires that applications send all requests for either input or output through the operating system. OS/2 acts as a "traffic cop" making sure that all communication between application programs and input/output devices occurs in an orderly manner. Each application is given its turn to communicate and potentially disastrous "collisions" are avoided. In the case of the printer, the first application to gain control of it is allowed to print an entire document before a second application can begin printing.

Privilege Levels

Even if application programs are constrained to operate within their assigned memory space and must go through the operating system to access I/O devices, there is still one important means by which they may affect each other. There are certain OS/2 commands that are intended to be used by the operating system to perform such functions as memory management and multitasking. If an application program were to contain such a command, it could have a major impact on the entire system.

In order to assure that no application program would ever be able to execute a command that could "bring down" the system or harm another application, the concept of *privilege levels* was added to the 286 chip. Privilege levels are used to control access to code areas and data areas as well as to certain critical instructions.

The 286 provides for four privilege levels, each one representing a level of trust. The most trusted level, level 0, has access to all areas and can execute all instructions. Generally, only system software would operate at this privilege level. After the operating system itself, the next most trusted code is the device drivers that provide access to the system's input/output devices. These drivers operate at privilege level 1. Privilege level 2 is reserved for various system extensions that may be added, and finally, the applications run at privilege level 3. Since application programs are the least trusted, they have the lowest privilege level and thus can do the least damage if they are faulty.

Protection of Data

Program data and program code are kept separate in different segments of the address space. The two types of information are treated somewhat differently by OS/2. OS/2 has several different provisions for protecting data. Every program running under OS/2 has an LDT as well as a GDT associated with it. Only data segments whose descriptors reside in one of those two tables can be accessed by the program. In addition, each descriptor contains a privilege level. Only programs having that privilege level or a higher privilege level (numerically lower) can access the associated data segment. Furthermore, a given privilege level may allow no more than read-only access to a data segment. Another check assures that, if a segment is written to, the new information does not go beyond the segment boundary.

Protection of Code

All the protections mentioned above for data segments also apply to code segments. In addition, the 286 prevents code segments from being modified during execution. It is acceptable for data to be modified during the running of a program, but modification of code is not at all desirable. Program code should never be designed to modify itself, since such code often leads to unforeseen, unpredictable conditions. If OS/2 ever detects that a program is attempting to modify itself, it assumes that the program is faulty and execution is terminated.

Another method of protecting code segments involves the privilege levels. A code segment at one privilege level cannot be activated by a code segment at another privilege level without the use of a special structure named a *call gate*. Call gates allow code at one privilege level to transfer control to code at a higher privilege level. With this device, application programs can call upon system software or system extensions to perform functions for them. The call gates themselves also have privilege levels. Programs can only invoke call gates that have lower privilege levels than the level of the calling program. By means of such a call gate, a program can only transfer control to code that has a higher privilege level. Call gates can never be used to transfer control to code that has a lower privilege level.

Input/Output Instructions

As we mentioned earlier, serious problems could occur if application programs were able to execute I/O instructions directly. Therefore, these 286 assembly language instructions can only be invoked by code that has the required privilege level. The privilege level required to utilize these instructions is set by the operating system, which is operating at privilege level 0, the highest privilege level possible.

This arrangement gives OS/2 the flexibility to decide the level of code that may perform various I/O operations.

System Critical Instructions

There are some instructions in 286 assembly language that control protected mode processes. These instructions cannot be trusted to any code other than the operating system itself, functioning at privilege level 0. For example the LGDT instruction loads the global descriptor table. An instruction of this power can only be trusted to the operating system.

MULTITASKING

Probably the most important single benefit of OS/2 is its ability to process multiple tasks concurrently in a protected and well controlled environment. Hardware included in the 286 architecture, along with OS/2 system code, implements multitasking efficiently and reliably.

Task Management

Overall execution is controlled by a priority-based time-slicing scheduler. The scheduler determines how frequently each task will run and for how long. Through its priority system, it is able to provide for the needs of applications with critical response time requirements as well as applications for which response time is not very important.

Under control of the scheduler, each application seems to run independently on its own computer. In reality, however, only one task is executing at any given moment. When the scheduler determines that the current task has run long enough, it initiates a *task switch*.

The system stores the *task state* in a data structure called the *task state segment* (TSS). The TSS contains all the information necessary to restart execution the next time this task becomes active. The TSS contains the address of the LDT associated with this task, as well as its segment register values, general purpose register values, instruction pointer, flags, and stack register values.

After OS/2 has stored the task state of the current task in the TSS, it loads the processor with the task state of the next task, which has been waiting for this moment in another part of the TSS.

The scheduler is not the only mechanism that can cause a task switch. The currently executing program can cause execution to switch away from itself to another task. However, in order for this type of switch to work, reference to the new task must already exist in either the active GDT or the active LDT. Remember from our discussion of protection that an application program can only reach those areas of memory that are referenced by an entry in either of the active descriptor tables.

Sessions, Processes, and Threads

OS/2 actually incorporates three distinct levels of multitasking. The highest level, and the only one visible to the user, is the session level. OS/2 interacts with the outside world at the session level. When you run applications under OS/2, each one is displayed on the screen as a session. Similarly, any input to the program, either from the keyboard or another input device, is sent to the appropriate session. The other two levels of multitasking, processes and threads, are subsets of a session. A session may have one or more processes, and a process may have one or more threads. Controlling the entire environment is the session manager.

The Session Manager

With the session manager, the user can control the execution of multiple concurrent tasks. It provides a screen oriented user interface and creates a work space for each task that you want to run. The Session Manager Screen (Figure 3.3), also known as the Program Selector Screen, lists these tasks, each one constituting a separate session. After OS/2 has been properly installed, it boots directly to the Session Manager Screen.

```
Update                                                    |   F1=Help

                            Program Selector

        To select a program, press ←, →, ↑, or ↓.  Then, press Enter.
             To select Update, press F10.  Then, Press Enter.

    ┌────────────────────────────┐      ┌────────────────────────────┐
    │   Start a Program          │      │  Switch to a Running Program│
    │   ─────────────────        │      │  ──────────────────────────│
    │                            │      │                            │
    │  • Introducing OS/2        │      │   • DOS Command Prompt     │
    │  • OS/2 Command Prompt     │      │                            │
    │                            │      │                            │
    │                            │      │                            │
    │                            │      │                            │
    │                            │      │                            │
    │                            │      │                            │
    │                            │      │                            │
    │                            │      │                            │
    └────────────────────────────┘      └────────────────────────────┘
```

Figure 3.3
The Session
Manager Screen

At this screen you can choose between three options. If you select the first option, "Introducing OS/2," the Session Manager starts a tutorial on OS/2. The other option on the left hand side of the screen, "OS/2 Command Prompt," starts an OS/2 mode session. If you select the option on the right hand side of the screen, "DOS Command Prompt," the Session Manager moves you into a new DOS mode session. You may select the "OS/2 Command Mode" option several times, since OS/2 supports multiple OS/2 mode sessions. Each time you select this option, a new OS/2 mode session will be started. On the other hand, only one DOS mode session is supported at a time.

After each OS/2 mode session is started, the name of that session on the session manager screen is changed from "Start a program" to the name of the application that is running in that session.

When execution in a particular session has been completed and you wish to remove that session, return to the Session Manager Screen and select the session to be removed. When the session has been selected by highlighting it and pressing Return, type the EXIT command, then press Enter. The screen will now show one less session.

Processes and Threads

It is possible to run multiple applications within a session. Each such application is called a *process*. A process is the execution of an application and also encompasses the ownership of any system resources associated with that execution. A process may consist of one or more *threads* of execution. Figure 3.4 gives an example of three independent processes executing concurrently within a session. Each is unaware that it is sharing disk space and processing cycles with the others.

Figure 3.5 shows a single process divided into three asynchronous execution threads. Each thread uses different devices and operates independently of the other threads to accomplish its part of the overall task. A thread is an execution path, and at any given instant in time, only one thread can be executing. This means that all other threads in the current process and in other processes, in the current session and in other sessions, are either blocked or waiting to run. Threads are assigned priorities that determine how often they will run.

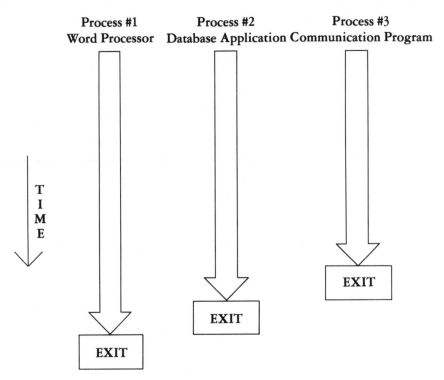

Figure 3.4
Multiple Independent
Processes

Data Sharing among Processes

We have just gone to great lengths to show how OS/2 protects one process from being affected by other concurrently executing processes. However, with some applications, you may want such processes to affect each other. At the very least, you may want two or more processes to have access to a common data set. OS/2 provides several mechanisms for such data sharing.

One way to make a data segment available to multiple processes is to put a descriptor of the segment into the GDT. All processes having a privilege level equal to or higher than the privilege level specified in the descriptor will be able to access the segment. Since all qualifying processes would access the segment through the same descriptor, they would all have the same access rights. This method should be used with care since any process with a sufficiently high privilege level has as much control of the data as does any other.

A more restricted form of data sharing involves giving two or more processes the same LDT. Only those processes with the shared

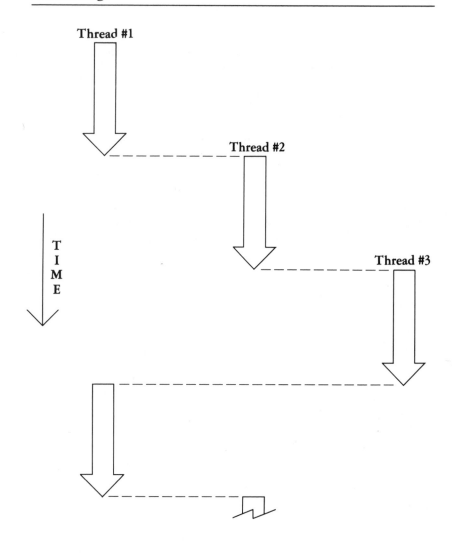

Figure 3.5
Multiple Execution
Threads within a
Single Process

LDT would have access to the shared data segment. The problem with this method is that processes which share the same LDT share all of their data. All processes involved would have the same access rights to all the data. This form of data sharing is only workable if all the sharing processes have been written to cooperate intimately.

Perhaps the best form of data sharing makes use of the device of *aliases*. Aliases are duplicate descriptors that are placed into the LDTs of all processes that need access to the shared data segment. Aliases provide a good deal more flexibility than do the sharing of descriptor tables. With aliases it is possible to specify exactly which segments are to be shared, and by which processes. It is also possible to ascribe different access rights and even different types to different processes. For example, one process may have read/write access to a particular segment while another has read-only access. Another segment may be considered a code segment (and thus unalterable) by one process, but a data segment by another.

Choosing a Multitasking Level

Programmers writing applications that make use of multitasking must decide whether to implement concurrent execution at the session, the process, or the thread level. It almost never makes sense to spread an application across two or more sessions. The OS/2 Session Manager is an example of such an application, but it is a special case. The overhead involved with a multisession application is high, and there is probably no advantage over a single session application that uses multiple processes.

If the multitasking elements of an application have a high degree of independence, or if they need to be protected from each other, use multiple processes within a single session. On the other hand, if the multitasking elements are small and execute for short periods of time, it is better to program them as multiple threads within a single process. The overhead involved with starting and stopping threads is much less than that needed to start and stop processes. In addition, threads can share data with less overhead than processes can. If two multitasking elements are closely related and need to share data, they should probably be programmed as threads rather than as processes.

Interprocess Communication

Having access to common areas in memory is not the only way that concurrently executing processes can communicate with one another. OS/2 provides several additional channels of interprocess communication. The simplest of these is the *pipe*. As the name implies, a pipe is a conduit of information from one process to another. In most cases, the two processes involved are unaware that they are connected by a pipe. As far as the source process knows, it is sending data to a file. As far as the destination process knows, it is receiving data from a file. Piping is actually a more general concept, and is used to convey information in single-tasking real mode applications as well as in a multitasking environment. We will revisit piping in a later chapter.

The second mechanism for interprocess communication is the *queue*. Queues allow faster transfers than pipes do, and they can handle larger amounts of data. While a pipe can transfer no more than 64K in a single operation, a queue is limited only by available memory. With a queue, the data is not actually copied, but resides in a segment shared by the involved processes, making transfer virtually instantaneous. In addition, a queue gives the destination process control over what information it will accept and in what order. Figure 3.6 diagrams the flow of information from the sending process to the receiving (or destination) process. The simpler pipe can deliver no less than all the data provided by the source process, and must do so in First-In-First-Out (FIFO) order.

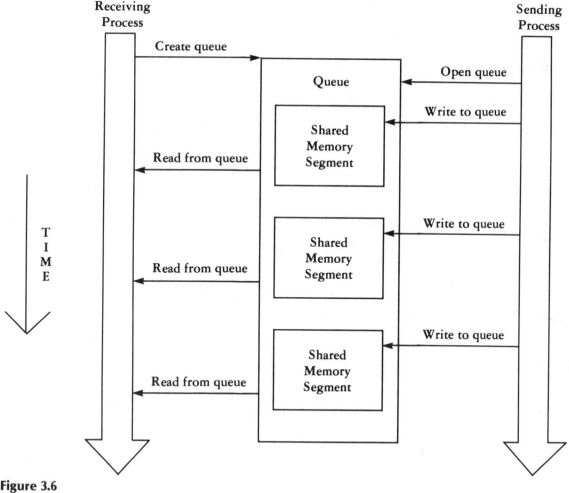

Figure 3.6
Sharing Data between
Processes Via a Queue

Semaphores, the third device used to facilitate interprocess communication, provide a form of arbitration among multiple concurrent threads or multiple concurrent processes. RAM semaphores, commonly used with threads within a single process, control access to system resources that can only be used by one thread at a time. System semaphores, used between processes, provide a similar function. They serialize inputs that they receive in parallel form, and they signal destination processes about the state of source processes.

Taken together, the various methods of sharing memory, combined with the use of pipes, queues, and semaphores, provide all the mechanisms for data sharing among concurrent processes that a programmer is likely to need. Application systems of considerable power can be constructed in such an environment.

SUMMARY

In this chapter we talked about some of the limitations of the 8088 architecture and of the DOS that was built around that architecture. We then covered the advanced design features of the 80286 microprocessor, specifically, its ability to run in protected mode and its ability to perform memory management. Protected mode operation is the basis for OS/2's multitasking capability. Memory management allows a machine running OS/2 to handle programs that require more memory than is physically available. Finally, the session manager is that part of OS/2 that is seen and used by the operator. It controls the execution of tasks, in both the DOS (real) mode and the OS/2 (protected) mode environments.

Chapter 4

Using Floppy Disks

OVERVIEW

The primary method of transporting new programs and data to a computer is via diskettes (floppy disks). Floppy disks are a handy form of removable on-line storage that can be readily exchanged between compatible computers. Floppy usage with OS/2 is somewhat complicated, however, since there are four distinctly different types of diskette that are supported by OS/2 with device driver code in the system BIOS. It is unlikely that your computer will be equipped with disk drives that are capable of accommodating all four types. In this chapter we will discuss how OS/2 uses diskettes, how to deal with the different types, and how to care for them and the disk drives that use them.

THE FOUR MAJOR FLOPPY DISK TYPES

OS/2 runs on the IBM PC-AT and with AT-compatible machines, such as Compaq and Zenith 286 and 386 machines, that have the same basic architecture. This means that OS/2 supports the two principal floppy drive types that are available on the AT, both the 5.25-inch 1.2Mb high-capacity diskette drive and the 5.25-inch 360K double-sided double-density diskette drive. These drives may be installed in the computer, or they may reside in a small cabinet of their own, connected to the computer via a cable.

OS/2 is always delivered on 1.2Mb media for such systems since the 360K floppies do not have enough capacity to contain all the code needed to boot OS/2 up for the first time.

The Personal System/2 Models 50, 60, and 80 all incorporate 3.5-inch floppy disk drives. These drives have a capacity of 1.44Mb. Accordingly, OS/2 for these machines is delivered on 3.5-inch floppies of the appropriate capacity.

An external floppy disk drive with a capacity of 720K may also be connected to either a PS/2 or to an AT type machine. OS/2 is capable of using this type of drive also. In fact, any of the four types of floppy disk drive may be connected to any of the OS/2-compatible systems as an external drive. OS/2 is capable of using any one of them or any mix of drive types.

HOW OS/2 USES FLOPPY DISKS

Just as floppy disks are the medium by which OS/2 system software is transferred to your computer, you will also receive most of your application software via floppy disk. Once your software has been safely copied to your system hard disk, you will not need to use floppies in the course of normal operation. (The exception is if you have created a DOS partition on your hard disk. In that case, you will need to insert a system floppy disk every time you want to boot OS/2.)

Once all your software is resident on your hard disk, floppies are useful for backing up selected information on your hard disk and for transferring files out of your system to be used on other computers. Floppies are not appropriate for backing up an entire hard disk, since floppy data transfer rates are relatively low and since an unacceptably large number of media changes would be needed to copy the entire contents of a 20Mb hard disk. Copying hard disks larger than 20Mb onto floppies is completely out of the question.

In Chapter 10 we will cover alternative backup methods in detail. It is critical to back up any and all important information stored on a hard disk. Although the reliability of hard disks has improved dramatically over the last several years, it is still all too possible to turn on your computer some fine morning and find that your information has been destroyed or irretrievably corrupted.

CARE AND MAINTENANCE OF DISKETTES

Floppy disks are susceptible to a variety of hazards, any one of which can render the disk unusable. Nothing is more frustrating than to rely on a backup floppy to recover a lost file, only to find that you cannot read your backup.

Since floppy disks record information by magnetizing small regions on the surface of a flexible platter of magnetic material, the data can be destroyed by placing the diskette into the presence of a strong magnetic field. Therefore, care should be taken to always keep floppy disks far removed from magnetic fields.

Another serious threat to floppy disks is contaminants on the surface of the disk. They interfere with the ability of the disk drive's read/write head to read the information recorded on the diskette. Contaminants range from dust particles to spilled coffee—anything that will adhere to the surface of the disk. If you suspect that a floppy disk is starting to be affected by contaminants, copy its information to another floppy before it fails completely.

Physical deformation of the floppy disk will also cause it to become unreadable. Mishandling can cause such a problem, as can extremes of temperature and humidity.

The answer to the foregoing litany of problems is to establish a habit of protecting your floppies before problems develop. Always store floppy disks in the protective envelopes provided by their manufacturer. Keep them in boxes that protect against dust and direct sunlight. Maintain them at room temperature. If you do subject a diskette to either extreme heat or cold, wait until it returns to room temperature before inserting it into a floppy disk drive and attempting to use it.

CARE AND MAINTENANCE OF FLOPPY DISK DRIVES

Floppy disk drives are fairly delicate devices. Several parts of the mechanism must be aligned to tight tolerances. It follows that such drives should not be subjected to any more shock and vibration than absolutely necessary.

Of course, care should also be taken to avoid contaminants that might adhere to the read/write heads. These heads contact the floppy disk itself while the disk is rotating at 300 rpm. At this speed, any foreign substance on a head could easily destroy the data the head passes over. Although there is no prescribed maintenance procedure for the user of floppy disk drives, it is possible for a qualified technician to clean the heads if they become dirty. If you start to experience problems reading or writing one of your diskette drives, consider taking it in for maintenance.

HOW DO FLOPPY DISKS WORK?

The floppy disk media, which is circular and rotates within a square protective envelope, is divided into a series of concentric tracks. Both the top and the bottom surfaces of the diskette are covered with magnetic material (iron oxide), and there is a separate read/write head for each side. The read/write head moves radially in and out with respect to the center of the diskette to access the various tracks. Each track is further divided into sectors. A sector contains the minimum amount of information that can be read or written at one time. Figure 4.1 diagrams the division of a typical floppy disk platter into tracks and sectors. Each of the different sizes and capacities of floppy disk will have a different number of tracks and/or sectors. However, the general scheme of the construction is the same in all cases.

The surface of the floppy disk platter is covered with a coating of magnetic material. The read/write head contains an electromagnet whose polarity is changed by a signal coming from the computer. When a binary 1 signal enters the head, the media directly beneath it is magnetized in one direction. When a binary 0 enters the head, the

Outer Edge
of Disk

A Sector
Boundary

A Typical
Track

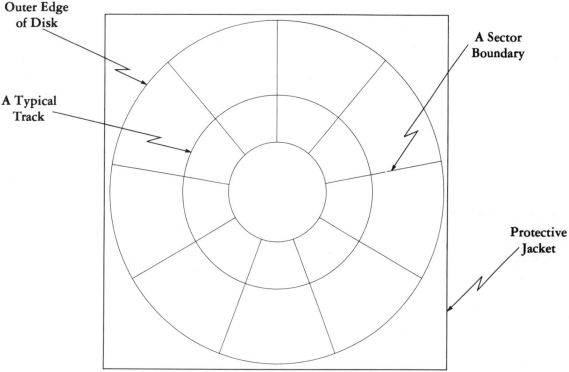

Protective
Jacket

**Figure 4.1
Floppy Media,
Showing Location
of Tracks
and Sectors**

media is magnetized in the opposite direction. In this way, a magnetic
map that corresponds exactly to binary data and program code that
reside in the computer can be built up on the diskette. Since the
timing of the reading and writing is exactly synchronized to the
rotation of the disk, data written to disk can be retrieved reliably with
a read operation. The read operation is the opposite of the write
operation. When writing, a voltage in the head causes the magnetization of the disk to change. In the case of reading, the magnetization of
the disk induces a voltage in the read head. This voltage is then
interpreted as a 1 or a 0 and sent back to the computer.

It is possible to protect diskettes that contain valuable data from
being inadvertently overwritten. This is done by applying a write-
protect tab over a notch in the edge of the diskette envelope (the

write-enable notch). When the write-protect tab is in place, the diskette is called a *write-protected diskette*. Your computer will not write to a write-protected diskette. If you ever want to change the data on a write protected diskette, merely remove the write-protect tab. The diskette can now be written upon. After making your change, you may want to reapply the write-protect tab to prevent further alteration. Often commercially developed programs are delivered on permanently write-protected diskettes. There should never be any reason to change the data on these diskettes, so the envelopes contain no write-enable notch, thus removing all possibility of accidental data destruction.

WHAT IS FORMATTING AND WHY IS IT NEEDED?

When a brand new floppy disk is placed into a floppy drive for the first time, it is not immediately usable. This is because the magnetic coating consists of a hodgepodge of magnetic domains, all oriented in a totally random fashion. As you would expect, the disk is unreadable. Surprisingly, it is also unwriteable. In order for data to be written in such a manner that it can be reliably retrieved later, the data must be placed down in strict relationship to *synchronization marks* that are already on the disk. These synchronization marks are actually the track and sector framework that we mentioned above. This framework must be put into place by formatting the diskette before it can be used.

Some diskettes that you can buy are preformatted at the factory. Others are not. Even if you buy the preformatted kind, it is a good idea to format them again on your computer. This will assure that there is no incompatibility between the operating system used at the diskette factory and the one running on your computer. Such an incompatibility may cause unreliable operation, and thus should be avoided.

THE FORMAT COMMAND

FORMAT is the OS/2 command used to structure a floppy disk into tracks and sectors. While it is structuring the disk, it is simultaneously checking the media for defective spots. Whenever it finds a defect, FORMAT *maps around* it, so that only good media is made available for the storage of data. If your system files reside in the root directory of your hard disk (drive C) and you wish to format a floppy disk installed in drive A, use the following command:

```
FORMAT A:
```

In addition to creating tracks and sectors, the FORMAT program also creates three special areas on the disk. The first reserved area is for the boot record. You may or may not wish to use a diskette as a boot disk for starting up OS/2. In either case, space for the boot record is reserved by FORMAT. Thus, even though you may not initially use a floppy for a boot disk, you may do so at a later time without reformatting. You have this option because room for the boot record is always reserved during the format operation.

The second area reserved on all floppy disks is the file allocation table (FAT). This table keeps track of the physical location on the disk of every piece of data written to it. It is a kind of map of the disk layout. Every time a file is written, changed, or erased, the FAT is updated to reflect the changes in the location of data.

The third item created by the FORMAT program is the directory. The directory keeps track of the name, size, and creation date of every file on the disk. Once space for the boot record, file allocation table, and the directory have been set aside, the rest of the formatted space on the disk is available for user data.

When you are formatting a diskette, there are a couple of options that you may wish to use. If you want to make the disk you are formatting into a boot disk, you may do so by specifying the /s parameter as part of the FORMAT command:

```
FORMAT A: /s
```

You now have the option of booting OS/2 from the hard disk, or from the new boot diskette that you have just created.

Another option you have when formatting is to specify a volume label for the diskette. After the format operation is complete, the computer prompts you as follows:

```
Type in an 11-character volume label, or press Enter.
```

If you press Enter, you are declining to specify a volume label. You may not care to identify this particular floppy disk. However, if you are formatting this floppy for a specific purpose, perhaps to hold the files containing all the letters you have written during the last month, you may want to specify an appropriate label, such as LETTERS.

After you have specified the volume label, FORMAT reports to you the number of bytes there are on the disk and the number available for use. The display looks like this:

```
1213952 bytes total disk space
1213952 bytes available on disk
```

If defective sectors had been mapped around, then the number of bytes available would be less than the total disk space. In the above example there were no defects, so the two numbers match.

Finally, the FORMAT program asks you if you would like to format another diskette. If you answer "Y" (for yes) it will repeat the above procedure. If you answer "N" (for no) you will exit the FORMAT utility.

CAUTION: One important thing to keep in mind is that the format utility wipes a diskette clean of *any* information that may be on it. Before you format your diskette, be absolutely sure that it does not contain any information that you want to keep. Once the formatting operation has begun, it is too late to retrieve any useful information from the disk.

THE DIRECTORY

We mentioned earlier that the FORMAT utility creates a directory after it has finished formatting a disk. This directory, called the root directory, is required in order for you to locate files on the disk. You have the option of creating additional directories, a topic that we will cover in Chapter 5. However, such additional directories, called *subdirectories*, are primarily used with hard disks. Floppy disks are small enough in capacity that in most cases there is no need to define subdirectories. The small number of files that comfortably fit on a floppy can usually be accommodated in the root directory without overcrowding the directory display.

The DIR command causes the display on the system monitor of the name of every file in the directory. In addition to the name of each file, its size in bytes and the date and time of its creation are shown. To display a directory of the files stored on the floppy disk installed in drive A, enter the following command:

    DIR A:

Since you have just formatted the floppy installed in that drive, the directory listing shown in Figure 4.2 is a rather short one. OS/2 warns us that no file was found.

The DIR command is actually a good deal more powerful than we have shown here. In Chapter 5, when we are exploring hard disks, we will cover the DIR command in considerably more depth. At this point, however, we see that the DIR command is the quickest and most reliable method of determining which files are stored on a floppy disk. Labels attached to the outside envelope of the floppy can lie, but the directory listing shown by the DIR command cannot. It shows exactly which files are present.

```
   OS/2        Ctrl+Esc = Program Selector              Type HELP = help
 [A:\]dir

 Volume in drive A has no label.
 Directory of A:\

 SYS0002: The system cannot find the file specified.

 [A:\]
```

Figure 4.2
Directory Listing of a
Newly Formatted
Diskette

COPYING FILES FROM ONE DISK TO ANOTHER

OS/2 contains three commands that mediate the transferral of information from one disk to another. They are BACKUP, COPY, and XCOPY. The BACKUP and XCOPY commands are primarily used when transferring data from a hard disk onto floppies. We will cover them later when we talk about hard disks. The COPY command is the most convenient tool for transferring individual files or groups of related files. We will discuss several of the main uses for this powerful command.

The COPY command works the same way, regardless of whether it is copying information between two floppy disks of the same size, two floppy disks of different sizes, or a floppy disk and a hard disk. Nonetheless, in each of these three situations, you must be aware of different concerns.

Copying between Two Identical Floppy Disk Drives

The simplest use of the COPY command is to copy information from one floppy disk (the source disk) to a second (blank) floppy disk of the same size (the destination disk). The second disk should be blank in order to be considered the same size as the source disk. If there are already files residing on the destination disk, they take up space that is thus unavailable for use in storing files from the source disk.

There are two main reasons for copying files from one floppy disk to another of the same size. The first reason is to transport information from one computer to another. If you write a program that is valuable to your company, you will probably want that program to be available on several if not all of the company's computers. The best way to disseminate the program is to copy it onto one floppy disk for each computer to which you wish to transport the program.

An example of this usage would be:

`COPY A:ledger.exe B:`

This command copies one file, named "ledger.exe" from the A floppy to the B floppy. The first command argument (A:ledger.exe) is called the source file specification. It consists of a drive identifier (A:), a filename (ledger), and an extension (exe). The destination file specification is shorter because only the drive identifier has been explicitly shown. The filename and extension are understood to be the same as the filename and extension in the source file specification unless they are explicitly shown to be different.

The second reason to copy information from one diskette to another of the same size is to create a backup copy. If you have a diskette containing valuable programs or data, it is wise to make an identical copy and put it in a safe place. For example, when you buy software on floppy disks, you should make identical copies of the distribution disks that you receive from the software vendor. Use your copies as working disks and place the original distribution disks in an off-site vault or other safe place. If your working disks become unusable, you can make another set by copying your originals again. It is unlikely that whatever misfortune caused your working disks to fail (power failure, operator error, fire, earthquake, etc.), will also affect your originals.

To copy all files from your primary floppy disk drive (the A drive) to your secondary drive (the B drive), as you would when making a backup copy, use the following command:

`COPY A:*.* B:`

The asterisk is a wildcard character that can stand for any character or any group of characters. As used here, the COPY command copies all files on drive A onto drive B. The question mark is another wildcard character. It can stand for any single character in a filename. The question mark is rarely used because the more versatile asterisk can be used in nearly all instances where a wildcard is needed.

Copying between Two Different Floppy Disk Drives

It is quite possible that a computer might have two floppy disk drives of different capacities. For example, you may have a PC-AT or compatible that has a 1.2Mb 5.25-inch drive and a 360K 5.25-inch drive. Another likely case would be a Personal System/2 Model 50 with an internally mounted 1.44Mb 3.5-inch drive and an external 360Kb 5.25-inch floppy disk subsystem.

In both of the above cases, one drive has substantially more capacity than the other. Use of the COPY command is just the same as it is with identical drives, except for the fact that you must be careful about one additional thing. When copying from the larger (meaning larger capacity, not larger diameter) drive to the smaller one, make sure that the files you are copying will fit on the destination disk. You may do this by listing a directory of the files to be transferred and comparing their total size in bytes to the amount of space free on the destination disk. If the size of the files is less than the amount of space free on the destination diskette, you may proceed with the COPY. If your destination disk does not have enough free space, you may have to perform the copy in segments rather than all at once. In the event any one file is larger than the space available on your destination diskette, you cannot use the COPY command to transfer the file. You will have to use the BACKUP command instead, which we will cover in detail in Chapter 10.

Copying between a *Floppy Disk Drive* and a *Hard Disk Drive*

Copying from a floppy disk drive to a hard disk drive presents different problems from the reverse operation. First let's consider what is involved in copying from a floppy to a hard disk, then look at copying from a hard disk to a floppy.

Floppy to Hard

Since the hard disk has so much more capacity than a normal floppy disk has, you may encounter a problem that you do not have to face when you copy from a smaller diskette to a larger diskette. Since a hard disk can hold such a large number of files, the directory listing becomes progressively less helpful as the number of files on the disk grows. To alleviate this problem, OS/2, like DOS before it, is organized into a hierarchical system of directories, each one of which is called a subdirectory. We will discuss hierarchical directories thoroughly in Chapter 5. Here we will just say that this kind of directory structure allows you to divide files into logical groups. Each subdirectory would contain a manageable group of related files. When copying files from a floppy disk to a hard disk, be sure they are copied into the appropriate subdirectory. As long as you limit the number of files that reside in a subdirectory, data stored on a hard disk is as easy to manipulate as data stored on a floppy disk.

Hard to Floppy

When copying files from your hard disk to a floppy disk, the main thing to keep in mind is that the files being copied must not take up more space than is available on the floppy disk. Before copying, make a directory listing of the files you intend to copy. The number of bytes taken up by each file is shown. Just as you did when copying files from a large floppy disk to a small one, make sure that the free space on the destination disk equals or exceeds the amount taken up by the files that are to be transferred.

EXERCISES

To help familiarize yourself with the commands we have discussed in this chapter, complete the following exercises.

1. Format a floppy disk using the FORMAT command. Use the proper syntax so that you do not erase all the data on your hard disk by mistake.

2. If you did not give your floppy disk a volume label when you formatted it, give it a label now using the LABEL command. If you did give it a label at format time, change that label with the LABEL command.

3. Place the OS/2 Diskette 1 in floppy drive A and display a directory of its files on the terminal screen.

4. Display a directory of only those files that have an extension of "exe."

5. Copy all files from the Program Disk to the root directory of your hard disk designated drive C. Display a directory listing of the root directory of drive C to verify that all the files were copied properly.

6. If you have a second floppy disk drive on your system, copy all files with an extension of "exe" from your program disk in drive A to a blank diskette in drive B. Display a directory listing of drive B to verify the copy operation was successful.

COMMON MISTAKES

It is possible to produce incorrect results if OS/2 commands are used improperly. Typing errors are one big cause of problems. Most typing errors result in an illegal command. When this is the case, the system displays an error message and waits for you to reissue the command in a corrected form. More dangerous is the case when a typing error transforms the desired command into an unintended but perfectly legal second command. The system will proceed to execute this unwanted command, perhaps with disastrous results.

One potential danger inherent in the COPY command is the fact that when you copy a file from one disk to another, OS/2 will copy it right on top of the file of the same name on the destination disk, if such a file exists. This is handy if you are updating an older version of the file with the latest one. However, if you get your source and destination confused and mistakenly copy the older version onto the most recent one, you will have lost all the work that you had put into the revision. Always take time to verify in your mind that your syntax is correct before executing a COPY command that might overwrite data that you wish to retain.

SUMMARY

Floppy disk drives are an integral part of nearly every computer that runs OS/2. Only certain network nodes and computers that incorporate some other type of removable media might possibly operate without a floppy. Generally, a floppy is needed to load OS/2 onto a system the first time. Thereafter, floppies are used principally to back up hard disk files.

OS/2 supports both 5.25- and 3.5-inch drives. Capacities of the drives offered by IBM range from a 360K 5.25-inch drive to a 1.44Mb 3.5-inch drive, with a couple of other capacities in between. Other manufacturers offer additional products, including a 10Mb floppy disk drive. These products are not supported by IBM device drivers, so the needed drivers are supplied with the drives by their manufacturers.

In this chapter we have described the use of the FORMAT, DIR, and COPY commands as they relate to floppy disks. These commands are essential for transporting OS/2 and other programs onto your system, keeping track of them and moving them from one disk to another. Additional features of these commands will be covered during our discussion of hard disks in the next chapter.

Chapter 5

Using Hard Disks

WHY A HARD DISK IS NEEDED

HOW DO HARD DISKS WORK?

PREPARING A HARD DISK FOR USE
  Low Level Format
  Partitioning
  Formatting

CHANGING THE CURRENT DISK DRIVE

HIERARCHICAL DIRECTORIES
  Creating a Directory (MKDIR)
  Changing from One Directory to Another (CHDIR)
  Removing a Directory (RMDIR)

COPYING FILES ONTO THE HARD DISK

MAKING A DIRECTORY LISTING

ACCESSING FILES THAT ARE OUTSIDE THE WORKING DIRECTORY
  PATH
  APPEND and DPATH

HARD DISK RISK FACTORS

HOW OS/2 USES THE HARD DISK FOR MEMORY MANAGEMENT

EXERCISES

COMMON MISTAKES
  Accidental Use of FORMAT
  Attempt to Remove Active Subdirectory
  Overwriting Files in Error
  PATH, APPEND, and DPATH Commands
  Back Up

SUMMARY

WHY A HARD DISK IS NEEDED

With a single-tasking operating system such as DOS, there are a number of useful applications that can be performed on a personal computer equipped with two floppy disk drives. However, a multi-tasking operating system such as OS/2 requires much more storage than is available on a pair of diskettes. For one thing, OS/2 itself is quite large. When the operating system is combined with such necessary items as a compiler, an assembler, and utility programs, floppy disks cannot hold everything needed. Even if they could hold it all, the slow performance of floppies would make using them a nuisance. Much time would be spent removing a floppy you have just used to make room for another which contains the code you will need to access next. Most importantly perhaps, application programs such as database applications, large spreadsheets, graphics applications, as well as speech and music synthesis require ever larger amounts of storage. Many such applications cannot be done at all without many megabytes of storage on line. Hard disks provide the only cost effective form of nonvolatile read/write memory currently on the market.

HOW DO HARD DISKS WORK?

In many respects, hard disks are similar to floppy disks, but there are important differences. Hard disk drives contain one or more permanently installed platters of rigid magnetic media. As with floppy disks, the magnetic properties of the platter are provided by a thin layer of magnetic material that coats the surface of the disk. Since the environment inside the hard disk's head disk assembly (HDA) is much cleaner and better controlled than the environment within a floppy disk envelope, the hard disk can safely rotate much faster than the floppy disk can. Typically a hard disk rotates at 3,600 rpm as compared to the floppy's 300 rpm rotation speed.

Like the floppy, the hard disk is divided into a number of tracks and sectors. On hard disks, however, the tracks are packed together much more closely, resulting in many more tracks full of data. In addition, each track holds more sectors than a floppy disk track does, increasing information density even more.

Another important difference between the hard disk and the floppy disk is that the hard disk's read/write head does not actually touch the rotating media as it does in a floppy. Instead it rides on a thin cushion of air that is dragged along by the rotating disk. As long as the disk is rotating above a certain critical speed, the head "flies" several thousandths of an inch above it on this so-called Bernoulli layer.

Reading and writing information on a hard disk is done in exactly the same way as we described for the floppy disk. Voltage changes in the read/write head induce magnetic polarity reversals on the surface of the disk, and vice versa. Since every important parameter of the hard disk is more carefully controlled than the corresponding parameters on the floppy disk are, information can be packed much more densely on a hard disk. This higher information density contributes greatly to the higher capacity of hard disk devices. Another factor is the fact that more than one platter can be enclosed within a single HDA. Current models contain as many as eight platters, each platter with its own set of read/write heads.

PREPARING A HARD DISK FOR USE

Before OS/2 can be installed on a computer system, the system hard disk must be prepared to accept it. This preparation is a multistage process, with each successive stage dependent on the completion of the previous stage. The first stage is so primitive that the user documentation does not even mention it. It is assumed that the hard disk user will never have to deal with a low level format.

Low Level Format

When a hard disk drive is first manufactured, the data platters within it are not able to accept data. The magnetic material coating the surface of the disk has not been magnetized in an orderly way. A pattern of tracks must be defined, and each individual bit must be located and set to a predetermined state as a first step toward turning the disk drive into a storage device.

This imposition of order upon the hard disk drive is achieved with a short program called a low level format routine. Be careful not to confuse the low level format operation, also called the primary format operation or the drive initialization, with the operation performed by the OS/2 FORMAT command. The FORMAT command puts a high level format onto the disk. We will discuss the high level format operation later in this chapter.

The main reason you should be aware of low level formatting is that it may enable you to salvage a hard disk drive that seems to be hopelessly damaged. There are occasions when the magnetic domains on a hard disk are scrambled in such a way that the disk is unreadable. If repartitioning the drive and performing a high level format does not restore the drive to health, it is possible that a low level format may yet revive it. Take your system to your dealer for the low level format operation. If even low level formatting does not return the disk to functionality, it is time to buy a new disk drive.

Partitioning

Once the low level format has been performed, the next step is to partition your hard disk. This is done with the FDISK command. You may use either the DOS FDISK command or the OS/2 FDISK command. If you intend to run DOS in one partition and OS/2 in another, it is probably a good idea to use the DOS version of the FDISK command.

The partitioning process creates one or more discrete areas on the disk drive. Each partition is identified by a letter of the alphabet. The partitions are considered to be logical (as opposed to physical) disk drives. Disk drives are identified with a two-character name that begins with a letter of the alphabet and ends with a colon. Since OS/2 does not distinguish between upper and lower case letters, you may use them both interchangeably. While the identifiers "A:" and "B:" are reserved for floppy disk drives, "C:" and above may be used to designate either logical or physical hard disk drives. Thus it would be possible to have a hard disk with two partitions, holding DOS and OS/2 respectively. These two logical partitions would be labeled "C:" and "D:". If a second physical hard disk were connected to the system and divided into two partitions, those partitions would be called drives "E:" and "F:".

If you want to boot directly from hard disk rather than from a boot floppy, copy the operating system files into drive C. You can perform this copying of system files automatically during the FOR-MAT operation by specifying the /s parameter in the FORMAT command line. At boot time, the computer's system startup logic first looks for a system disk in floppy drive A. If no floppy is installed in drive A, the startup logic next attempts to boot from the hard disk partition designated drive C. If it does not find system files in either place, the startup logic will issue an error message and terminate.

Even though multiple partitions may exist on the same physical hard disk, there is no communication across partition boundaries. Each partition is an entity unto itself. Thus you may have a DOS partition that has no way of knowing that an OS/2 partition exists on the same disk. Conversely, the OS/2 partition would be unaware of the DOS partition.

Formatting

After a hard disk has been partitioned, the next step is to give it a high level format with the FORMAT command. The format operation creates a directory and file allocation tables on the disk. The directory and file allocation tables keep track of where files are located on the disk. Whenever a disk is formatted, the directory and file allocation tables are wiped clean. Any information that had been present on the disk is no longer recoverable, since it can no longer be located on the disk.

The same FORMAT command that is used to format hard disks is also used to format floppy disks. Hopefully, you will only have to format your hard disk once. However, it is likely that you will be formatting floppy disks frequently if you use them for archiving, backup, or for transporting files between computers. Since the same command is used to format hard disks as is used to format floppies, it is possible that a keyboard error might cause you to format your hard disk when you meant to format a floppy. To avoid this traumatic occurrence, you may want to write a small batch file to format floppies. In this way, every time you call the batch file, you can be sure that the proper syntax will be used. In Chapter 9 we will discuss batch files in detail.

If you have booted your system from drive A, and the FORMAT command is resident on that drive, to format your hard disk (drive C), simply enter

`FORMAT C:`

If you do not specify an argument, the format command will prompt you for one. There is no default argument.

The format command will lay down tracks and sectors on your hard disk, map around bad spots, and reserve areas for a boot record, a FAT table, and a directory.

Since it is much faster and more convenient to boot from your hard disk than it is to boot from a floppy disk, you will probably want to transfer your system files to the hard disk. If the system files are present in the root directory of the hard disk, your computer will automatically boot itself from the hard disk after it has checked to see that no floppy disk is installed in drive A. You can make the hard disk bootable at format time by specifying the /s parameter when you format it. The proper syntax is

`FORMAT C: /s`

The format command will next allow you to specify a volume label if you wish. You may not wish to bother, since you probably have only one hard disk on your system. You will have little opportunity to get your disk volumes confused.

Next, FORMAT will report to you the total number of bytes of space on the disk and the number available for use. It will then ask you if you wish to format another disk. To exit the program respond with an "N."

> WARNING: If you accidentally format a disk that already contains data, you will not be able to recover that data. This situation is much more serious than it is in the case of a floppy disk. Instead of losing only a few hundred thousand bytes of data, you could wipe out hundreds of megabytes with a single word. Be *very* careful how you use the FORMAT command.

CHANGING THE CURRENT DISK DRIVE

Immediately following bootup, the currently active disk drive, called the current drive for short, is the boot disk. It contains the system files and could be either a hard disk or a floppy disk drive. If you want to execute a program that resides on some disk other than the boot disk, you must change the current disk drive to the drive containing your program. This is easily done. If your current drive is presently drive A and you want to switch to drive C, simply enter "C:" followed by a carriage return. To switch back to drive A, merely enter "A:", again followed by a carriage return. Regardless of the number of disk volumes you have on line, you can access any one of them by entering the appropriate drive designation letter followed by a colon.

HIERARCHICAL DIRECTORIES

Today's hard disks, with capacities that vary all the way from 20Mb to several hundred megabytes, can hold hundreds or even thousands of files. If all those files were listed in the same directory, retrieving files would become a frustrating and time consuming chore. Many errors would be made. For instance an existing file could easily be over-written by a new file with the same name, merely because you forgot that you already had a file with that name.

To avoid problems like those given above, OS/2 is structured so that multiple directories can be created. You can put a relatively small number of related files into each directory. This greatly speeds up file access and at the same time reduces the chance of misapplying or deleting unrelated files. Directories can be structured in a hierarchical manner. This means that files that are very closely related can all be placed in a single directory. Files that are less closely related can be placed in related directories, called subdirectories. Figure 5.1 shows the way a typical disk might be divided into directories and subdirectories.

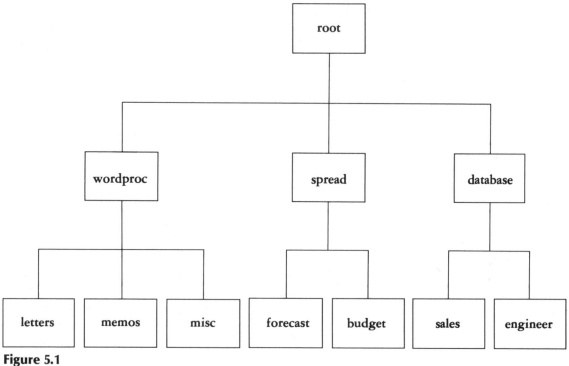

Figure 5.1
Diagram of a Typical
Directory Structure

The root directory should be reserved for system files. All applications should reside in subdirectories of their own. In the figure, there are three main functional areas: word processing, spreadsheet analysis, and database management. Each gets its own corresponding subdirectory: "wordproc," "spread," and "database" respectively.

Each subdirectory can, in turn, have subdirectories of its own. In the example in the figure, "wordproc" has three subdirectories, while "spread" and "database" both have two. You may give a directory as many subdirectories as you wish, but it is not a good idea to create too many. If you do, you will have traded the problem of an unmanageable number of files for the equally difficult problem of an unmanageable number of directories. Try to achieve a balance between the number of directories and the number of files in each directory.

Creating a
Directory
(MKDIR)

To create a subdirectory, use the MKDIR (make directory) command. For example to create the word processing directory shown in Figure 5.1, issue the following command:

```
MKDIR C:\wordproc
```

OS/2 will create a subdirectory named "wordproc" directly beneath the root directory on your C drive. To create a subdirectory of a subdirectory, proceed in a similar way. We can create the "letters" subdirectory of the "wordproc" directory by typing

```
MKDIR C:\wordproc\letters
```

We may proceed in this manner to create all the subdirectories shown in Figure 5.1. The argument "\wordproc\letters" is called a path specification. Paths are the routes you take to travel from one subdirectory to another.

If we are operating in protected mode, the MKDIR command is somewhat more powerful than it is in real mode. In real mode, we can create only one subdirectory with each MKDIR command. In protected mode, we can create multiple subdirectories with a single MKDIR command. In protected mode we can create both the "wordproc" and the "letters" subdirectories with a single command:

```
MKDIR C:\wordproc \wordproc\letters
```

To create a subdirectory of the working directory (the one you are currently operating in), it is not necessary to include information about the location of the new directory. Thus, if the working directory is "wordproc" and you want to create a new subdirectory named "memos," you may use the following syntax:

```
MKDIR memos
```

For convenience, an abbreviated form of the MKDIR command is also available. It works exactly the same as the longer form. The only difference is that it is a little easier to enter from the keyboard. To create the "misc" subdirectory while operating from the "wordproc" working directory you need only enter

```
MD misc
```

In protected mode you could create all three subdirectories of "wordproc" very efficiently by making "wordproc" the working directory, then typing

```
MKDIR letters memos misc
```

You may well ask, "How do I change the working directory?" It is done with the CHDIR command.

Changing from
One Directory to
Another (CHDIR)

The CHDIR command changes the working directory to the directory you specify. If the working directory is currently "\wordproc\misc" and you wish to change to the "\spread\forecast" directory, use

```
CHDIR \spread\forecast
```

You can verify that the working directory has indeed been changed by issuing the CHDIR command without an argument, like this:

`CHDIR`

OS/2 will respond by displaying the current working directory on your screen.

There are some shortcuts available with the CHDIR command. First of all, you may abbreviate CHDIR to CD. The shorter form of the command is interpreted in exactly the same way as the longer form. Secondly, you need not specify the entire path of the new working directory if your current working directory is either immediately above it or below it.

If you are in the "database" directory shown in Figure 5.1, you can reach the "sales" subdirectory by entering

`CHDIR \database\sales`

However, since you are already in the parent directory "database" you can move directly to the child directory with

`CD sales`

By the same token, if you are in the "sales" directory, you may change the working directory to "database" by typing

`CD \database`

Since "database" is the parent of the "sales" directory that you currently occupy, and since any subdirectory can have one and only one parent, you may also go directly to the parent with the command

`CD ..`

Removing a Directory (RMDIR)

As time goes on and your computing needs change, you may find that an application that you have used in the past is no longer valuable to you. To make room for files of more immediate value, you will want to delete the obsolete files from your disk. Even after you erase all the old files, however, the directory that contained them will remain. In order to keep your disk from becoming cluttered with old empty directories, OS/2 provides a command for removing unwanted directories. It is the RMDIR or RD command. The syntax to use with it is exactly the same as the syntax you used with the MKDIR command. Remember, however, that the RMDIR command will only work on an empty directory. If the directory you are attempting to remove has one or more files in it, the RD command will have no effect. An error message will be returned to you instead. To remove the empty subdirectory "engineer" from the directory tree shown in Figure 5.1, issue the command

`RMDIR \database\engineer`

If you tried to remove the "database" directory now, OS/2 would not cooperate, since the "sales" subdirectory still exists. You must remove all files and subdirectories contained in a directory, before the directory itself can be removed. First remove the empty subdirectory "sales"

```
RD \database\sales
```

Now that the "database" directory is completely empty, it too can be removed.

```
RD \database
```

An important point to remember is the fact that the working directory cannot be removed. If you have just deleted all files from the working directory and now you want to remove it, you must first change directories with the CHDIR command. If you make the root directory your working directory, you will be able to easily remove any empty subdirectory.

COPYING FILES ONTO THE HARD DISK

In Chapter 2 we showed how to copy the OS/2 system files to the hard disk in order to get OS/2 up and running. Application systems are copied to the hard disk in much the same way, but with a slight bit of additional complication. For best results, each application should be isolated in its own subdirectory or group of subdirectories. Many applications will create these subdirectories for you automatically with an installation program. Others will not, so you must create the subdirectory yourself.

Let us return again to the typical installation shown in Figure 5.1. Let's say that you have a word processing application stored on floppy disk. In addition you have several floppies containing the text files of business letters you have written over the last year, a floppy full of memos you have sent, and a diskette containing other miscellaneous text files. You want to place all this on your hard disk, where it will be more easily usable.

The required procedure is straightforward.

1. Create the needed subdirectories.
2. Copy the data on each floppy into the appropriate subdirectory.

Starting with the root directory as our working directory, we first create the directories:

```
MD wordproc
MD spread
```

```
MD  database
MD  \wordproc\letters
MD  \wordproc\memos
MD  \wordproc\misc
MD  \spread\forecast
MD  \spread\budget
MD  \database\sales
MD  \database\engineer
```

In OS/2 mode, we can create multiple subdirectories with a single MD command. We could create the same set of directories with just two MD commands. If we had used shorter directory names, we could have done it with a single command. The syntax is:

```
MD wordproc spread database \wordproc\letters \wordproc\memos
\wordproc\misc \spread\forecast \spread\budget \database\sales
```

```
MD  \database\engineer
```

Next we insert the diskette containing the word processor program in the A drive and copy all the program files to the proper subdirectory in the hard disk. We can copy all the files at once by using wildcard characters (asterisks) instead of specifying each individual file name. The following form of the COPY command will achieve our objective:

```
COPY  A:*.*  C:\wordproc
```

This copies all files on the floppy disk inserted in the A drive into the "wordproc" subdirectory on hard disk volume C. By successively inserting the appropriate diskettes and performing the corresponding COPY commands, we can copy all our files from floppies to our hard disk quickly and efficiently. The letters are transferred by inserting the diskettes that contain them and typing

```
COPY  A:*.*  C:\wordproc\letters
```

After changing diskettes, the memos are copied over in the same manner:

```
COPY  A:*.*  C:\wordproc\memos
```

In turn, insert the proper diskettes and issue the following commands:

```
COPY  A:*.*  \wordproc\misc
COPY  A:*.*  \spread
COPY  A:*.*  \spread\forecast
COPY  A:*.*  \spread\budget
COPY  A:*.*  \database
COPY  A:*.*  \database\sales
COPY  A:*.*  \database\engineer
```

At this point our complete word processing, spreadsheet, and database systems have been copied to the hard disk. Before we start executing our applications, however, let's discuss a few handy tools for keeping track of the files contained in each directory, and for accessing material in directories other than the working directory.

MAKING A DIRECTORY LISTING

We covered the basic usage of the DIR command in Chapter 4. It works the same way on hard disks as it does on floppy disks, but the presence of subdirectories adds a dimension to the syntax. In addition to specifying the drive identifier of the drive we wish to investigate, we also must specify the path that leads to the subdirectory of interest. To get a directory listing of the contents of the "memos" subdirectory shown in Figure 5.1 we would issue the following command:

```
DIR C:\wordproc\memos
```

Only the files contained in that specific subdirectory would be listed on the screen, along with a tally of the number of files contained in the subdirectory. In this way we can focus on the contents of each subdirectory without having to consider the files contained in other subdirectories on the disk.

ACCESSING FILES THAT ARE OUTSIDE THE WORKING DIRECTORY

There are a number of good reasons for keeping related files in different directories. For instance, if you put a major application like a database management system together with all its databases into the same directory, you might have an unmanageably large number of files.

Another problem is encountered when you mix program files and data files together in the same directory. Program files rarely change, while data files change constantly. To be protected from damaging data loss in the case of a system failure, program files need to be backed up only once in a great while. However, data files that change often must be backed up often. Since it is much more convenient to back up entire directories than it is to specify files individually, it makes sense to separate programs from data by placing them in different directories.

If the programs and the data are in different directories, how can they interact? OS/2 provides three commands that allow you to specify paths of linkage between directories. Once a link to another directory has been established, OS/2 will extend its search for a file beyond the working directory to all the other directories specified by these path setting commands.

PATH

The PATH command is familiar to many, because an analogous command exists in DOS. It instructs OS/2 to search other directories for command files. For example, in the directory tree shown in Figure 5.1, a user whose working directory is "wordproc" may wish to use a command that is located in the "database" directory. Rather than copy the file, which creates needless duplication and wastes disk space, we can access the command file by issuing a PATH command of the following form:

    `PATH \database`

Multiple paths can be specified with a single command if desired, with arguments separated by semicolons. Any time you want to know what the current path setting is, you may find out by issuing a PATH command without an argument, like this:

    `PATH`

OS/2 will display the current path setting.

APPEND and DPATH

There are many occasions when you may want to access files in other directories that are not command files. You may, for instance, wish to operate within the directory that contains your application's program files and access data files that are stored somewhere else. There are two commands that allow you to access noncommand files in the same way that the PATH command allows you to reach command files. The syntax is the same as that used by the PATH command. Both commands have identical syntax and identical function. The difference lies in the fact that the APPEND command functions only in DOS mode while the DPATH command functions only in OS/2 mode.

So, when operating in DOS mode, a combination of the PATH and the APPEND commands gives you access to any file in any subdirectory without changing your working directory. In OS/2 mode, the combination of PATH and DPATH gives you similar access to any needed files.

HARD DISK RISK FACTORS

Although hard disk drives give you much faster access to much more information than floppy disk drives can give you, they are a mixed blessing. Hard disk technology has some distinct drawbacks.

One such drawback is the fact that hard disk media is typically not removable. Your disk drive is chained to the computer within which the disk is installed. In order to transport the data away from your computer, you have to copy it to another storage medium. Floppy disks, on the other hand, are very portable and a convenient vehicle for transporting information from one computer to another.

Another drawback is related to one of the hard disk's greatest strengths, its tremendous capacity. Since the hard disk allows us to store as much as several hundred megabytes of data on a single disk, we are greatly tempted to place all of our important data upon it. This is tantamount to putting all of our eggs in one basket. This is dangerous. Your inadvertent failure to specify the proper argument while performing a FORMAT command could wipe out all of that data in the twinkling of an eye. There are other operator errors that could destroy large amounts of your data. Since all of your information is in one place, it is vulnerable to a host of threats. It is imperative to back up hard disk data regularly. We will make specific recommendations about backup in Chapter 10.

HOW OS/2 USES THE HARD DISK FOR MEMORY MANAGEMENT

When OS/2 is operated in OS/2 mode, you can use the virtual memory feature. Virtual memory allows you to run a single program or a group of concurrently executing programs that are larger than the amount of system memory installed in the system. This is possible because only the currently active segments of the applications are kept in RAM. Infrequently used parts of the programs are kept on hard disk. When one of these segments is needed, the memory management feature of OS/2 swaps the program segment that is least likely to be needed again soon out of RAM. After space has thus been recovered, the memory manager swaps the new segment into RAM. This entire sequence is performed automatically and goes largely unnoticed by the user. The system operates as if it has a much larger memory than it actually does. In this way, that portion of the hard disk that has been allocated for memory management becomes a part of the system memory.

For this speed-critical application, you want your system to have the fastest hard disk subsystem possible. Look for subsystems that offer low average access times, a high transfer rate, track buffering, and, where possible, disk caching. Track buffering refers to disk drives that incorporate enough RAM to hold an entire track of data. Whenever the operating system asks for a sector of data from the hard disk, the entire track containing that sector is stored in the track buffer. There is a good chance that another sector from that track will be needed soon, particularly if a sequential read of a long file is being made. If so, these subsequent accesses will proceed at RAM speed rather than at the much slower disk speed. Disk caching is another technique that involves placing the most active disk data into a special RAM. Whenever data in this RAM area is accessed, the average response time of the system is reduced accordingly. However it is done, optimizing the performance of the hard disk subsystem is a major consideration on any system that uses OS/2's virtual memory capability.

EXERCISES

1. With the root directory of your hard disk as the working directory, create a subdirectory named "testdir1".

2. Make "testdir1" the working directory and verify that you have successfully changed directories by causing OS/2 to display the current directory name.

3. Copy the file print.com from the root directory to "testdir1".

4. Display a directory listing of "testdir1", showing the presence of print.com.

COMMON MISTAKES

Accidental Use of FORMAT

A common error is to accidentally format the wrong disk. The worst form of this error is to format your hard disk when you intended to format only a floppy diskette. Actually, a hard disk should almost never be formatted. Only if a major failure causes the hard disk to become unusable should formatting it be considered. On the other hand, formatting floppies is a common occurrence. Since the command for formatting your hard disk and the command for formatting a diskette are so similar, it is easy to get them confused and format the wrong device.

A solution to this problem is to write a small program called a batch file that restricts the FORMAT operation to floppies only. You can write this program, named "flopform.bat", as shown below:

```
COPY con flopform.bat/a
FORMAT A:
^Z
```

The program is written directly from the console at the OS/2 system prompt. The first line instructs OS/2 to copy from the console to a program named "flopform.bat." The "/a" indicates that the program is in the form of an ASCII file. The second line is the actual FORMAT command. Since it explicitly specifies that the A drive is the one to be formatted, there is no danger of accidentally formatting any other drive. The "^Z" on the third line is the symbol displayed when you depress Ctrl-Z. Ctrl-Z creates an end-of-file marker and signifies the end of the program. After you enter the Ctrl-Z, OS/2 writes the program into the working directory of the current disk.

Now, whenever you want to format a floppy disk, you may do so in complete safety by issuing the command

FLOPFORM

Your batch file will call the restricted form of the FORMAT command and you can proceed with the format operation without having to think carefully about what you are doing. The diskette stored in the A drive is the only part of your storage system that can be affected.

Attempt to Remove Active Subdirectory

A bothersome but not particularly dangerous mistake is to try to remove a subdirectory that is not completely empty. If the subdirectory contains as much as one file or one subdirectory, OS/2 will refuse to remove it, emitting a cryptic error message instead. Actually, this is a safety feature. It prevents you from obliterating files that you may want to retain. You must explicitly delete all files and remove all subdirectories from the directory of interest before you can remove the directory with a RMDIR command.

Overwriting Files in Error

When copying files from one disk to another, remember that the COPY command copies the specified files from the source disk onto the destination disk. If some of the files that already exist on the destination disk have the same names as files being copied over from the source disk, the source disk files will supercede and replace the original destination disk files. They will be written right on top of the existing destination disk files. You must be careful that you do not copy an older, less complete, or erroneous copy of one of your files over the top of a newer, more complete and correct copy of the same file. If you do make such a copy, you will be back with your old version, and all the changes and improvements you had made between the two versions will have been lost.

PATH, APPEND, and DPATH Commands

You may want to set your working directory as the one that contains your application's data. In order to execute the application, you will need to set a path to the application program itself. If the program is in the form of a single command file, the PATH command will provide a sufficient link. However, if the program needs to access other subsidiary files, such as overlays or message files, PATH is not enough. These noncommand files are not made accessible by the PATH command. In addition, you must set another link with the APPEND command if you are operating in DOS mode, or with the DPATH command if you are using OS/2 mode. One of these commands is required to allow you to access noncommand files across directory boundaries.

Back Up

Since hard disk media is typically nonremovable, it is constantly at risk of erasure, either by operator error, deliberate malice, or equipment failure. An all too common mistake is to fail to back up hard disk data often enough. The consequences of this mistake can be anywhere from annoying to devastating. If your business depends on your computer data, back up often.

SUMMARY

Because of the size of OS/2 and the applications that run under it, many megabytes of on-line storage are needed. The best combination of speed and capacity at the lowest price is delivered by hard disks. Hard disks store data on the surfaces of rigid metallic disks in the form of tiny magnetized regions, each representing a single bit of information. By spinning rapidly under electromagnetic read/write heads, the disks are able to transfer data to and from the computer at high speed.

In this chapter we have discussed how to set up hard disks for use with OS/2. We have also covered the manipulation of the files that reside on those hard disks. The file manipulation commands and operators apply equally well to files that reside on floppy disks.

We briefly covered the low level formatting and partitioning of a hard disk. These fundamental operations should only have to be performed once in the life of a hard disk. Next we discussed the high level formatting of hard disks.

Like floppy disks, hard disks must be formatted before they can be used to store information. Once a disk has been formatted, it can be divided up into subdirectories that reflect the needs of the user. The user can set up as many or as few subdirectories as desired, and may organize them in a hierarchical structure that reflects the relationships between the groups of the files that they contain.

Files can be copied from one disk to another or from one subdirectory on a disk to another subdirectory on the same disk. Usually, however, it is not wise to make multiple copies of the same file on a single disk. It is better to maintain a single file, then set paths to it from the other subdirectories.

Much of the risk associated with a hard disk has to do with the fact that a tremendous amount of your data is all concentrated in one place. Add to that the fact that the hard disk is probably more vulnerable to damage from shock and vibration than any other part of your system. It is wise to keep multiple copies of your data on backup media, and to update the backups as often as the data changes significantly. If you use your data every day, you should perform a backup every day.

OS/2 uses a portion of the hard disk as a swapping area for the virtual memory feature. Virtual memory gives you the advantages of having a much larger system memory than is physically present, without the high cost that such a massive memory would normally entail.

Chapter 6

Creating, Copying, and Deleting Files

INTRODUCTION

Computer information is stored on floppy disks and hard disks in the form of files. A *file* is a collection of related information that can be drawn upon by a program running on a computer. Some files are themselves programs or parts of programs. Other files contain data that is used by a program. Now that we have discussed the basic organization of floppy and hard disks, it is time to describe in greater detail how the files stored on these disks are manipulated.

In this chapter we will cover how to move files from one disk to another and from one place on a disk to a different place on the same disk. We will also discuss methods to rename files and to remove them from a disk.

CREATING FILES

There are several ways to create files. We touched on one of them briefly in the last chapter when we created the small program "flopform.bat." To create this program we used one form of the multitalented COPY command. Let's take another look at our use of the COPY command in that program.

```
COPY con flopform.bat/a
```

If we were to translate this command into English, it would say, "Copy the following program code directly from the console (con) to a file named 'flopform.bat' in the working directory on the current disk. By the way, this file is an ASCII file (/a)."

Thus, one way of creating a file is to use the "COPY con" form of the COPY command. However, this method is only suitable for very short programs. Once a command line has been entered, it can no longer be edited. If you make a mistake, you will have to reenter the entire program from the beginning. For any program longer that a few lines, it makes sense to use a different method of file creation.

The most frequently used tool for creating programs is the text editor. A simple editor named Edlin is included with OS/2. Edlin is a real mode line editor. As the name implies, Edlin can only be used in real (or DOS) mode, and allows you to edit one line at a time. You may prefer to use a screen editor or a word processor in screen editor mode. With these more visually oriented file creation tools, you can view the file you are creating a screenful at a time, ranging back and forth at will to make changes.

Some language interpreters, such as the Microsoft BASIC interpreter, are themselves capable of supporting file creation. You may enter a BASIC program directly from the console, edit those lines that need correction, then execute the program directly. When you are satisfied that the program is functioning properly, you can save it to disk. This can all be done without the help of a text editor or other file creation tool. Alternatively, you could create your BASIC program with a text editor, load it into the interpreter, and execute it. A program that contains the same code will function the same way, regardless of how it was created.

A third possible method of file creation is by an application program. BASIC and other programming languages allow file creation. Thus programs written in these languages have the power to create files. You can write a program that creates files.

You can also use existing programs that create files. Thus, word processing programs can allow you to create text files, spreadsheet programs can allow you to create spreadsheet data files, and database manager programs can allow you to create database files. Other kinds of programs create other kinds of files.

MOVING FILES

Once a file has been created, you will need to store it. Even after a file has been stored, it is quite possible that you will need to move it from one place to another. The COPY command, which we have used several times already, is the primary tool used for moving files around the system.

Moving a File from a System Device to a Disk

This use of the COPY command is already familiar. We have seen how to use it to transfer a file from the console device to a disk. The syntax,

```
COPY con A:flopform.bat/a
```

causes the subsequent program lines to be copied into a file named "flopform.bat" on the diskette inserted into floppy disk drive A. To copy the same batch file into a subdirectory named "\utility" on your hard disk, type

```
COPY con C:\utility\flopform.bat/a
```

Moving a File from a Disk to a System Device

The COPY command works equally well at copying files in the other direction. Issue the command

```
COPY A:flopform.bat con
```

The contents of the file will be displayed on the console screen. In the same manner,

```
COPY A:flopform.bat prn
```

causes the contents of the file to be printed out on the system printer.

Moving a File from One Disk to Another Disk

Probably the most common use of the COPY command is to copy files from one disk to another. You may want to copy new software from a distribution diskette to your system hard disk. You may want to back up hard disk files on one or more diskettes. Finally, you may wish to copy files from one diskette to another diskette. All of these operations can be accomplished by the COPY command, and all with the same syntax. The only difference between commands is the form of the arguments that specify drives.

Copying from Floppy Disk to Hard Disk

To copy all batch files from the working directory of the diskette in floppy drive A to the working directory of hard disk drive C, you would enter

```
COPY A:*.bat C:
```

In the source argument (A:*.bat) we have specified both the drive designator and the names of the files to be copied. In the destination argument (C:), we have specified only the drive designator. Since the filenames have not been specified in the destination argument, the names are assumed to be the same names that appear in the source argument. The result would have been the same if we had specified the destination explicitly, thus:

```
COPY A:*.bat C:*.bat
```

Copying from Hard Disk to Floppy Disk

To copy files in the reverse direction, merely reverse source and destination arguments. To copy all batch files in the working directory of the hard disk to the working directory of the diskette installed in drive A, the command is:

```
COPY C:*.bat A:
```

To copy files from any directory in drive C to any directory in drive A, add the appropriate path specification to the command syntax. For example, to copy all text files stored in subdirectory "\wordproc\ memos" on the hard disk to subdirectory "\text" on the diskette in drive A, type in the command,

```
COPY C:\wordproc\memos\*.txt A:\text
```

With this command, all the text files will be copied to floppy and given the same name they had on the hard disk. When copying from a larger capacity disk to a smaller capacity disk (as in this case), always make sure ahead of time that there is sufficient room on the destination disk to hold all the data to be copied. If there is not enough room on the destination disk, an incomplete copy will be made.

Copying from One Diskette to Another Diskette

If you have two diskette drives on your system, you can copy files directly from one floppy to another. Even if you have only one floppy drive, you can still copy files from one diskette to another. It just requires a bit more work. To copy from one floppy drive to another, the procedure is the same as we have already covered. Only the drive designator is changed. So, to back up the text files that were just copied from the hard disk to the diskette in drive A, we may use the following command:

```
COPY A:\text\*.txt B:
```

(This command assumes that a subdirectory named "\text" already exists on the B diskette.)

Surprisingly, we use this same syntax even if there is no physical B drive present on the system. If there is only one floppy disk drive installed on a system, OS/2 will change the designator of that drive back and forth between A and B as needed. So in the case of the current example, OS/2 would instruct you to insert the source diskette in the floppy drive. After it has read a block of data, OS/2 instructs you to insert the destination disk in the drive. It then writes the block of data it has just read onto the destination disk. OS/2 then instructs you to insert the source disk again so it can read another block of data. The diskette drive alternately assumes the identities of drive A and drive B until all the specified files have been copied in their entirety. This procedure works but is quite tedious. As a shortcut, copy the files from the source floppy into an empty directory on your hard disk. Then insert the destination diskette into your floppy drive and copy the files from the hard disk to the destination floppy. The entire operation is accomplished in two simple steps.

SHORTCUT: To copy files from one diskette to another on a system with only a single floppy drive, create a "scratch" directory on your hard disk and copy all your source files to it in a single operation. Then insert your destination diskette into the drive and copy the files from the hard disk to the floppy in a second operation. Finally, erase the files from "\scratch."

Copying Files from One Directory to Another on the Same Disk

Since you can access any file in any directory on your hard disk from any other directory by setting a path with the PATH, APPEND, and

DPATH commands, there is little reason to copy commands from one directory to another on the same disk. However, there may be some occasions for such an operation. For example, you may want to move a file from its current directory to one that contains related files that should all be backed up together. Other reasons might be to consolidate files from several directories into one or to disperse files from one directory into several. The COPY command creates a duplicate of the existing file in the new directory. Later you can erase the original version if you wish with the DEL command.

When copying from one directory to another on the same disk, you may use syntax like that shown here:

```
COPY C:\spread\forecast\project.asc C:\wordproc\memos\project.asc
```

This form of the copy command will work correctly no matter what disk is the current disk and no matter what directory is the working directory. However, it is quite a long command. We can take shortcuts if the current disk is drive C, and even more shortcuts if the working directory is either the directory specified in the source argument or that specified in the destination argument. So if the working directory is indeed the "\spread\forecast" directory on drive C, we could perform the same copy by typing

```
COPY project.asc \wordproc\memos
```

Where the drive is not specified, the default is the current drive. Where directory is not specified, the default is the current directory. If filename is not specified in the destination argument of the COPY command, the default assumption is that the filename is the same as the filename specified in the source argument.

> SHORTCUT: When using several commands (such as COPY) that use path specifications, switch the default directory so that it is either the source or the destination directory. Then you need not type that path specification repeatedly while issuing commands.

As we have seen, the COPY command is a very powerful tool for duplicating files. It can also be used as a method of changing the name of a file, as we shall see in the next section.

COPYING AN ENTIRE DISKETTE

The DISKCOPY command is used for copying the contents of one floppy disk onto another. It is a very specialized command with only one purpose, which is in strong contrast to the flexible and highly general COPY command.

COPY may be used to transfer files between floppy disks and hard disks, or between floppy disks of differing capacities. COPY has the ability to change the filenames of the files it copies. COPY can concatenate multiple source files into a single destination file. COPY doesn't care if there are already files residing on the destination disk; it will deposit copied files anywhere on the destination disk where it can find enough room.

DISKCOPY cannot do any of those things. It knows nothing of files, but rather operates at a primitive level. DISKCOPY creates a byte-for-byte mirror image of the source diskette on the destination diskette. One of the disadvantages of this type of copying is that the copying operation does nothing to reduce the problem of fragmentation. After a disk, either floppy or hard, has been in use for a while, it becomes fragmented. Obsolete files are erased, leaving holes of available disk space interspersed with areas that contain active files. As you create new files they are written into these holes. If a file outgrows the particular hole it started in, the new part of the file is placed in the next available hole. Soon active files are strewn all over the disk in small chunks. This fragmentation slows down processing significantly, since the read/write head must do considerable seeking back and forth across the disk to read the entire file.

> HINT: Eliminate fragmentation at regular intervals by copying your fragmented disk to a freshly formatted disk of comparable capacity.

If you use the "COPY A:*.* B:" syntax, all the files on the A disk will be copied to the B disk as complete, unbroken files in one contiguous stream of data.

The DISKCOPY command should only be used when you must make a physically exact copy of your original diskette. In all other circumstances, use the COPY command.

RENAMING FILES

The RENAME command is specifically designed to allow you to change the name of a file. The name of a file can also be changed by the COPY command while the file is being copied from one place to another.

Using the COPY Command to Change the Name of a File

Since the COPY command gives us the opportunity to specify the filename of the destination file in a copy operation, it is possible to specify a filename that is different from the source filename. There are a number of circumstances under which you might want to change a filename when the file is copied. For example, if you are copying a file to a floppy to give to someone else, you may want to give it a more descriptive name than you used on your own disk. An example of such a COPY is

```
COPY C:\wordproc\memos\memo27.txt A:budget89.mem
```
Of course, this operation still leaves the old copy of the file at its original location with its original name. Now you have two files in two different places, with two different names, but which contain identical information.

Renaming Files with the RENAME Command

There will be times when you do not want to create a renamed duplicate of a file. You just want to rename an existing file. The RENAME command provides the means to rename single files or groups of files. To RENAME a single file, just specify the location and name of the file, then specify the new name as shown in the following example:

```
RENAME C:\spread\forecast\project.asc task.txt
```
File "project.asc" in the "forecast" subdirectory of the "spread" directory has been renamed to "task.txt". The location of the file may not be changed with the RENAME command, only the filename.

Suppose you have a group of files, each relating to a different project, named "projecta.asc", "projectb.asc", etc. You can change them all to the "task" nomenclature with a single RENAME command as follows:

```
RENAME C:\spread\forecast\project*.asc task*.txt
```
The file that had been "projecta.asc" is now "taska.txt". Similarly, "projectb.asc" is now "taskb.txt", "projectc.asc" is now "taskc.txt", and so on. We could change the filename but leave the extension unchanged by using slightly different arguments,

```
RENAME C:\spread\forecast\project*.* task*.*
```
With this command, the filename "projecta.asc" would be changed to "taska.asc" and the other filenames would be changed in the same manner.

An abbreviated form of the RENAME command is also accepted by OS/2. In every case above where we used the RENAME command, we could have used REN with equal effectiveness. Either form of the command works equally well.

ERASING FILES

To keep obsolete files from being confused with active files and to keep disks from filling up, we must have a way of erasing unwanted files. For this purpose, OS/2 provides the DEL command, also known as the ERASE command. The DEL command works in both DOS and in OS/2 mode, but the syntax is slightly different in the two operating environments. In DOS mode, only one file specification may be included with the DEL command. In OS/2 mode, multiple specifications may be included, allowing simultaneous deletions from different directories on different drives. In the next section, this ability of the OS/2 mode version of the DEL command is described in detail.

Erasing Groups of Files

You may use wildcard characters (* and ?) to cause the deletion of groups of files. For example, if you had the following files in the "\finance" directory,

```
budget.77
budget.78
budget.79
budget.80
budget.81
budget.82
```

you could erase those that contained records from the decade of the 1970s with the command,

```
DEL \finance\budget.7?
```

CAUTION: Whenever you use wildcard characters in a DEL command, there is a chance you might inadvertently erase files that you did not intend to erase. Always verify the scope of retrieval of a wildcard character with the DIR command before using it to remove files with the DEL command.

For instance you may have a series of magazine articles that you want to delete, stored in a subdirectory. They have such names as "article1.txt", "article2.txt", etc. You could erase them all quickly by issuing the command,

```
DEL arti*.*
```

To be safe, however, you run a quick directory first:

```
DIR arti*.*
```

To your surprise, the directory contains an unexpected entry.

```
article1.txt
article2.txt
article3.txt
article4.txt
artifact.txt
article5.txt
article6.txt
article7.txt
```

A paper you had written on Stone Age artifacts also resides in this directory. To retain the paper while removing the articles, you need to modify your DEL command slightly to

```
DEL artic*.*
```

RULE: Always verify the scope of a multifile deletion by first displaying a directory with the same file specification that you intend to use in your DEL command.

In OS/2 mode it is possible to erase multiple files with a single command, even when wildcard characters are not used. This feature is most useful when you want to delete several files whose names have nothing in common, or when the files reside in different disks or directories. For example,

```
DEL A:budget.83 C:\wordproc\memos\memo27.txt C:\scratch\*.pix
```

This command will delete a budget file from the A floppy, a memo from the word processing area of the hard disk, as well as all files with an extension of "pix" from the scratch directory of the hard disk.

Erasing All Files in a Directory

Sometimes you may wish to remove everything in a directory from your disk. To delete everything in the working directory, use the command,

```
DEL *.*
```

Since this is a fairly drastic operation, OS/2 gives you a chance to reconsider. It displays the query, "Are you sure (Y/N)?" on the display screen. If you respond by entering "Y," it will proceed with the deletion. If you enter "N," it will abort the operation. Once all the files in a directory have been deleted, the directory can be removed, using the RMDIR command as we discussed in Chapter 5.

EXERCISES

1. With the root directory of your boot disk as the working directory, create a batch file named "director.bat" using the "COPY con" form of the COPY command that displays the working directory on the screen.

2. Use the COPY command to copy an ASCII text file from one of your disks to the system printer (PRN).

3. Use the RENAME command to change the name of your batch file "director.bat" to "filelist.bat".

4. Create a subdirectory named "\scratch" on your hard disk and copy all the files in the root directory of your boot disk into it. Use the DIR command to verify that they were all transferred.

5. Erase all the files in subdirectory "\scratch" and use the DIR command to verify that they are gone.

COMMON MISTAKES

Attempting to Copy More Data Than the Destination Disk Can Hold

A problem that often occurs when copying from a hard disk to a floppy disk, or from one floppy disk to another, is insufficient room on the destination disk. Before copying to a floppy disk, use the DIR command on the destination disk to see how much free space is left. Then display a directory of the files you intend to copy to make sure that the space they require is less than the space available on the destination disk.

Deleting Too Many Files through Use of Wildcard Characters

When erasing unwanted files, care must always be taken to ensure that valuable files are not accidentally deleted along with the unwanted ones. Before issuing a DEL command that incorporates wildcard characters, always display a directory using the same file specification. If an unexpected file appears in the directory, you will know how to change the file specification such that your DEL command will delete only the files you want it to.

Perpetuating Fragmentation by Copying Files with DISKCOPY

Do not use the DISKCOPY command for normal archiving or file transfer purposes. It perpetuates the fragmentation of your files, contributing to poor disk performance. Use COPY instead.

SUMMARY

In this chapter, we have discussed the basic operations of creating files, moving them around, renaming them, and deleting them. Mastery of these "housekeeping" chores is an essential prelude to the actual use of OS/2.

Chapter 7

Operating on Files

INTRODUCTION

In this chapter we discuss OS/2 file naming conventions as well as the basic tools available for sorting and moving files. Operators that allow multiple commands to be combined into a single command line allow complex operations to be executed quickly and easily.

We have seen that the drive designators assigned to hard disks and to floppy diskettes tell OS/2 where to go when it wants to read or write data to a storage device. In much the same way, all the input and output devices have unique designators that identify them to OS/2. Table 7.1 lists the names of input/output devices other than disks and gives a brief definition of each.

Table 7.1
Designators of
Input/Output Devices

Designator	Device
CON:	The console device, consisting of the video display and the keyboard
COM1: or AUX:	The first asynchronous communications port
COM2:	The second asynchronous communications port
LPT1: or PRN	The first line printer or parallel port
LPT2:	The second line printer port
LPT3:	The third line printer port
NUL:	The null device; used for testing purposes only

As is true for disk drive designators, device names all end with a colon. The only exception is the PRN device name, which contains no colon. Unlike the disk drive designators, in which the colons are mandatory, for most uses the colons in the other device designators are optional.

IDENTIFYING FILES

We have already alluded many times to the fact that information is stored on disks in units called *files*. Each file is a collection of related information. Some files are program files which are sequences of instructions that are executed by your computer. Other files are data files, which contain information that may be accessed by program files during the course of execution. In either case, every file stored in a single directory on a disk must have a unique name. If two or more files were to have the same name, OS/2 would not be able to tell which one was wanted when that filename was requested. Consequently, OS/2 will not allow two files with the same name to coexist in the same directory. Two files with the same name, residing in different directories, are allowed since the total filename, including path information, of both files would be unique. Thus, the following two files could both reside on hard disk C:

```
C:\sales\report.txt
C:\market\report.txt
```

However, if you attempted to create a second file named "report.txt" in the "\sales" subdirectory of drive C, where one such file already existed, OS/2 would not allow the creation. Instead, it would simply overwrite the first file with the new one. You must keep track of the names of files that already exist in a directory before creating or copying a new file into the directory. You could easily destroy a valuable existing file by overwriting it with a new file that happens to have the same name.

Filenames consist of two parts, separated by a period. The first part, called the *root name*, can be from one to eight characters long. The second part, called the *extension*, is optional. If used, it can be from one to three characters long. All of the alphanumeric characters are legal characters for filenames, as are certain special characters. The following special characters are legal:

```
!@#$&()-{}'_
```

All other special characters and all control characters (such as Esc and Del) are illegal and may not be used in filenames.

Certain *reserved words* may not be used as the root name part of a filename. For example the names of the I/O devices are reserved words. Thus, such filenames as "con.txt," "prn.doc," or "com1.exe" are not legal. If you tried to write to files with these names, you would write to the console, the printer, and the asynchronous communications port respectively, instead. After OS/2 interpreted the root name as a device rather than as a disk file, it would ignore the extension. This characteristic of OS/2 is potentially dangerous, because you may believe you have successfully copied a file to disk, when in fact you have not. You have only copied it to an output device that does not store it for future use.

Besides avoiding the use of reserved words in filenames, you should also be aware that certain commonly used extension names have become standardized. Whenever possible, you should use the standard extensions on your files. They will help to remind you what kind of file you are using. In addition, many programs expect these common extensions and will not work properly without them. Table

7.2 gives many of the most commonly used extensions and the type of file to which they belong.

Table 7.2
Commonly Used File
Name Extensions

Extension	Associated File Type
.ASM	Assembly language source file
.BAK	Backup file
.BAS	BASIC language program file
.BAT	Batch file
.COM	Command file, an executable program file
.DAT	Data file
.DBF	Database file used with dBASE DBMS
.DIF	File format used to exchange data between different programs
.DOC	Document (text) file
.EXE	Executable program file
.LET	Letter (text) file
.LST	Program source listing
.MAP	LINKER map file
.NDX	Index file for a database
.OBJ	Object code file
.OVL	Program overlay file
.PRN	Program listing file
.SYS	Device driver or system configuration file
.TMP	Temporary file
.TXT	Text file
.WKS	Lotus 1-2-3 worksheet file
.WK1	Lotus 1-2-3 Release 2 worksheet file

REDIRECTION

OS/2 assumes that the system console is the primary input/output device. Unless you tell it otherwise, it will look for input to come from the console keyboard and it will send output to the console screen. If you want OS/2 to accept input from somewhere else, or to send output to somewhere else, you may use the *redirection* facilities built into OS/2.

The less-than sign ($<$) is OS/2's symbol for input redirection. Input redirection causes input for a command to come from a file rather than the keyboard. The greater-than sign ($>$) represents output redirection. Output redirection causes the output from a command to go to a disk file or to a device other than the screen. For example, you may have a list of names in a file named "names.uns". You are constantly appending new names to the file, which is not in any particular order. You can use input redirection to pass the names through a SORT filter, then output redirection to write the sorted names into a new file. The syntax would be:

```
SORT < names.uns > names.srt
```

If you redirect output to a file that already exists, the existing file will be overwritten with the new information. All the old information will be lost. You may wish to merely append the new information to the old, rather than replacing it completely. In this case use the double greater-than sign ($>>$) for output redirection. It works just like the single variety except in the case where the destination file already exists. If the double greater-than is used, the new output is appended to the existing file. If the single greater-than is used, the new output replaces the existing file.

FILTERS

SORT is one of three *filters* available under OS/2. The other two are FIND and MORE. A filter is a command that reads an input, processes it in some way, then outputs it to the terminal screen. As we have seen, we may use output redirection to send the output to places other than the screen.

The SORT command accepts data from an input source, sorts it in alphanumeric order based on the first character of each record, then displays the result on the screen. A couple of options are available, one allowing you to sort in reverse alphanumeric order and another causing the sort to start at any specified character in the record. Thus, if you wanted to sort the records of the file "names.uns" by zip code and the zip code always started at the ninety-eighth character of each record, the syntax to use with the SORT filter would be

```
SORT /+98 < names.uns
```

To perform the same sort in reverse zip code order (starting with the highest zip code rather than the lowest),

```
SORT /r /+98 < names.uns
```

The MORE filter is most useful to people who view output on the screen. Most terminal screens only display 24 lines of output before they start to scroll the earliest lines off the top of the screen. In many cases, information of interest will scroll off the screen before you can examine it. If you take information that is headed for the screen and pass it through a MORE filter, it breaks the display up into screen-sized chunks. After one full screen has been displayed, the scrolling stops and the word "—More—" appears at the bottom of the screen. You may now take as much time as you wish to study the information on the screen. When you are ready to proceed, strike any key on the keyboard (e.g. the space bar) to cause the next screenful to scroll up. In this way, you can examine very large displays at your own pace. To inspect the unsorted names file a screenful at a time, you could use the following syntax:

```
MORE < names.uns
```

The third filter, FIND, searches for occurrences of a specific string of text in one or more files. Several options are available. The primary option is to display all lines of text that contain the specified string. Another possibility is to display all lines of text that do not contain the specified string. A third option is to merely display the number of lines that contain the specified string, and the last option appends relative line numbers to the display. This last option allows you to easily locate those lines that contain the specified string. As an example, suppose you wanted to know whether the unsorted "names.uns" file contained anyone named Satterthwaite. The following command would quickly give you the answer:

```
FIND "Satterthwaite" names.uns
```

A differentiation is made between upper and lower case letters within the search string, so you must capitalize in the search string those letters that are capitalized in the file being searched.

PIPES

Pipes are logical structures that take the output of one command and direct it to the input of another command. To use a pipe, separate two commands with the pipe symbol, a vertical bar (|). We can use input and output redirection, filters, and pipes to manipulate data in very useful ways. For example, first sort the unsorted names file using input redirection and the SORT filter:

```
SORT < names.uns > names.srt
```

The sorted file can now be displayed on the terminal a screenful at a time, using a pipe and the MORE filter:

```
      TYPE names.srt | MORE
```
The same display could be obtained in a single command as follows:
```
      SORT <names.uns | MORE
```
In this case, a sorted copy of the file is not saved on disk.

OS/2 MODE GROUPING SYMBOLS

The redirection, filters, and piping that we have just discussed are features that are available in DOS mode of OS/2 as well as OS/2 mode. They are also available under DOS. In OS/2 mode some additional operators are available to us for file manipulation. They are called the *OS/2 mode grouping symbols*. We will now describe each of these symbols and their operation.

The AND Symbol (&&)

The AND symbol, denoted by the double ampersand (&&), is related to the logical AND operator of symbolic logic. The AND operator is used to separate two commands on the same command line. First the command to the left of the AND symbol is executed. If the execution is successful, then the command to the right of the symbol is executed. On the other hand, if the command on the left fails to execute properly, no attempt will be made to execute the command on the right. Stated logically,

> If, and only if, the command on the left executes successfully,
> will execution of the command on the right be attempted.

The OR Symbol (||)

When the OR symbol (||) separates two commands, either the one on the left will be executed or the one on the right, but never both. This operator is related to the Exclusive OR operator of symbolic logic. First the command to the left of the OR operator is attempted. If execution is successful, the command on the right is not attempted. Conversely, if execution of the command on the left fails, then execution of the command on the right is attempted. Stated logically,

> If, and only if, execution of the command on the left fails,
> will execution of the command on the right be attempted.

The Command Separating Symbol (&)

The command separating symbol controls an operation that is close to our intuitive perception of the meaning of the word "and." When two commands are separated by the command separating symbol, they are both performed, starting with the command on the left. Stated logically,

Execution of the command on the left is attempted, then, regardless of the result, execution of the command on the right is attempted.

The Escape Symbol (^)

The escape symbol (^) is used to remove any special significance of the character that immediately follows it. In effect, it says, "Treat the immediately following character as if it were an ordinary character, with no special significance." For example, you may wish to use the greater-than sign to mean "greater-than" rather than signifying output redirection. If so, merely place an escape symbol in front of the greater-than sign, and OS/2 will treat it as an ordinary character.

COMMAND GROUPING

You can put a large number of commands on a single line, connected by redirection symbols, pipes, or OS/2 mode grouping symbols. If the various operations are not executed in the exact order that you expect, you may get unpredictable and misleading results. To prevent this kind of problem and remove the possibility of ambiguous results, OS/2 executes operations according to a fixed hierarchy, and also allows you to group commands by surrounding them with parentheses. The command hierarchy is as follows:

^	Escape symbol
( )	Command group parentheses
<,>,>>	Input and output redirectors
|	Pipe symbol
&&	AND symbol
||	OR symbol
&	Command separator

In any complex command line, the escape symbol is always executed first, if it is present. Next the commands within the parentheses are executed, and so on. If there is ever any doubt in your mind as to the order in which commands will be executed, include parentheses to insure that the order you desire is the order that will be taken. For example, you may want to run a directory to see if the sorted names file exists. If it does not, then create it by sorting the unsorted names file:

```
DIR names.srt ‖ TYPE names.uns | SORT > names.srt
```
Due to the hierarchy of the operators, the redirection will be performed first, then the pipe, followed by the OR. This order of execution will give us the desired result.

However, just to make sure, we can add parentheses to make it obvious at a glance that the expression will be evaluated properly:
```
DIR names.srt ‖ (TYPE names.uns | SORT > names.srt)
```
Only if the file "names.srt" does not exist in the current directory will OS/2 sort the unsorted file and write it into a new file named "names.srt". If we had grouped things otherwise, say like this:
```
(DIR names.srt ‖ TYPE names.uns) | SORT > names.srt
```
OS/2 would have sorted the error message telling us that the system cannot find file "names.srt" right in with all the names in the "names.uns" file—an unsatisfactory result, to say the least. Whenever executing two or more commands on a single line, double check to make sure the commands will be executed in the proper order.

EXERCISES

1. Run a directory of the root directory of your boot disk, redirecting the output of a DIR command so that the output appears on your system printer instead of the console.

2. Print out the directory again, but this time sort it with a SORT filter before routing it to your printer.

3. Print out the directory again, but this time specify that you want to sort on Column 10. The result will be a directory sorted by extension rather than by root name.

SUMMARY

Unique designators for all disk drives as well as unique designators for all input and output devices attached to the system were covered. Every device connected to an OS/2 system must have a unique identifier. As an extension of that concept, every file on the system must also have a unique identifier. That identifier, the filename, must meet certain format criteria and must not contain any reserved words.

Redirection of input and output allows information to be routed to places other than the system console. Filters and pipes allow the results of one command to be processed and then passed to another command for additional manipulation. Multiple operations can be performed on a single command line through use of redirection, pipes, filters, OS/2 mode grouping symbols, and the command grouping symbol (parentheses).

Chapter 8

Configuring an OS/2 System

CUSTOMIZING THE OPERATING ENVIRONMENT
DEVICE DRIVERS
BUILDING AN EXAMPLE CONFIGURATION FILE
EXERCISES
SUMMARY

CUSTOMIZING THE OPERATING ENVIRONMENT

Different people will be running different kinds of application software on their OS/2 systems. Because of these different applications, they will require different resources from the system. OS/2 gives you the opportunity to specify a great deal about the environment within which you will be operating. This specifying is done with the system configuration file, named "config.sys".

When an OS/2 system is first turned on, the ROM BIOS executes a series of tests and initializes system logic. Next, the BIOS looks for a boot sector, initially on the first floppy disk and then on the first fixed disk. If an OS/2 boot sector is present on either of those two disks, the OS/2 system code is loaded, and it assumes control. After OS/2 is completely loaded and initialized, execution switches from real mode to protected mode. Finally, if a file named "config.sys" is present in the root directory of the boot drive, it is read, and the commands it contains are executed. If a system configuration file is not present, OS/2 sets the configuration variables to default values.

Table 8.1 contains the commands that could be contained in a "config.sys" file, along with a brief description of the function of each.

In addition to the commands listed in Table 8.1, OS/2 also allows the commands FILES and LASTDRIVE to reside in "config.sys," but it ignores them. These commands are functional under DOS, but have no effect under OS/2. Let us examine each in a little bit more detail. In the following discussion and throughout this book, command syntax elements enclosed in square brackets ([ ]) are optional.

Table 8.1
System Configuration Commands

Command	Arguments	Function
BREAK	ON or OFF	In DOS mode only, determines whether or not OS/2 will check the keyboard for Ctrl-Break
BUFFERS	"a number"	Determines the number of buffers in memory that will be allocated to disk I/O
CODEPAGE	xxx[,yyy]	Lets you decide what character set will be used; different code pages support the character sets of different languages
COUNTRY	"country code"	Determines conventions for time, date, and currency

continued

Table 8.1
System Configuration
Commands (continued)

Command	Arguments	Function
DEVICE	"filename"	Specifies the path and filename of a device driver to be installed
DEVINFO	"device type, code page table name"	Provides OS/2 with information about an I/O device that will be affected by code page switching
FCBS	"a number"	In DOS mode only, specifies the number of file control blocks that can be concurrently open
IOPL	YES or NO	Input/Output Privilege Level, controls access to I/O devices
LIBPATH	"path"	Specifies the location of the Dynamic Link Library
MAXWAIT	"# of seconds"	Maximum time a process can go without getting CPU time
MEMMAN	SWAP or NOSWAP MOVE or NOMOVE	Enables or disables memory management options
PRIORITY	ABSOLUTE or DYNAMIC	Specifies type of scheduling
PROTECTONLY	YES or NO	Selects mode of operation
PROTSHELL	"filenames"	Specifies the name(s) and location(s) of the DOS and OS/2 mode command processor(s)
RMSIZE	"kilobytes"	Determines the amount of memory dedicated to DOS mode operation
RUN	"a filename"	Starts a process immediately after system initialization is complete
SHELL	"a filename"	In DOS mode only, loads and starts the top level command processor
SWAPPATH	"a path"	Specifies the location of the swap file
TIMESLICE	"milliseconds"	Sets the minimum and maximum time slices that can be allotted to a process
THREADS	"a number"	Sets the maximum number of threads the system can concurrently support
TRACE	ON or OFF or "a number"	Enable or disable the system trace or specify a major event code between 0 and 255
TRACEBUF	"a number"	Set the trace buffer size with a number between 1 and 63

BREAK

Purpose: Checks the keyboard for a Ctrl-C whenever a system call is issued. The BREAK command allows the operator to terminate execution of a program before it comes to a natural completion.

Syntax: BREAK = on
      or
      BREAK = off

Default: BREAK = off

Environment: DOS Mode only. (PROTECTONLY = no, or there is no PROTECTONLY command in the "config.sys" file.

Remarks: There are times when you may want to break out of a program before it finishes executing. A new program that has not been completely debugged may take an unexpected (wrong) path, and there is no sense continuing. When BREAK = ON, OS/2 will check the keyboard every time the executing program attempts to use one of the resources of OS/2 to see if Ctrl-C has been depressed. If it has, execution of the current program will be immediately terminated. When BREAK = OFF, OS/2 will check for the depression of Ctrl-C only when it is reading information from the keyboard, or sending information to the screen or the printer.

    Since frequent checks for Ctrl-C may noticeably slow down program execution, you may want to run with BREAK = Off if you are running only proven, "bullet proof" software. On the other hand, if you are not sure about the soundness of your programs and speed is not a top priority with you, you will probably prefer to run with BREAK = ON.

Example: When running code of questionable validity, check often for a Ctrl-C signal from the keyboard by specifying:

    BREAK = on

BUFFERS

Purpose: Specifies the amount of memory (number of buffers) that OS/2 will set aside for disk I/O at system boot time.

Syntax: BUFFERS = x (where x is a positive integer from 1 to 99)

Default: BUFFERS = 3

Environment: DOS Mode and OS/2 Mode

Remarks: The more information that can be stored in memory buffers, the fewer times the system must go to the disk for needed data. Since disk storage is much slower than system memory, allocating more buffers generally speeds up system throughput. The default value of three buffers is woefully inadequate for any serious work. In a hard disk based system, 20 buffers are reasonable. The standard IBM OS/2 installation program sets BUFFERS = 30. Experiment with BUFFERS = 20, BUFFERS = 30, BUFFERS = 40, etc. to find the optimal setting for the type of applications you typically run. Each buffer takes up 512 bytes of memory. Thus, 40 buffers would take 20K away from your application program space. If you are close to using all the memory that you have, you may want to limit the number of buffers that you allocate in your "config.sys" file.

Example: For a system used primarily for word processing, it is reasonable to allocate buffers as follows:

```
BUFFERS = 20
```

CODEPAGE

Purpose: Selects the character sets that will be used when outputting information to the screen or the printer.

Syntax: CODEPAGE = xxx[,yyy] (where xxx and yyy are three digit system codes that specify the primary and secondary code pages)

Default: CODEPAGE = 437,850 (unless a COUNTRY command in the "config.sys" file specifies otherwise)

Environment: DOS Mode and OS/2 Mode

Remarks: A *code page* is a table containing the character set or sets that you will be using. The available code pages are:

Page Number	Character Set
437	United States
850	Multilingual
860	Portuguese
863	Canadian-French
865	Nordic

Code page 850 is noteworthy in that it contains the *common character set* also known as *character set ID 697*. The common character set meets the known character requirements of the following languages:

Belgian French	Norwegian
Canadian French	Portuguese
Danish	Spanish
Dutch	Latin-American Spanish
Finnish	Swedish
Flemish	Swiss French
French	Swiss German
German	UK English
Icelandic	US English
Italian	

These languages are used by most of the nations in the Western Hemisphere and in Western Europe.

Note: The DEVINFO command is used with the CODEPAGE command to facilitate code page switching. It specifies characteristics of devices that are affected by a code page switch.

Example: To use the character set that contains all French Canadian punctuation marks, issue the command,
```
CODEPAGE = 863,850
```

COUNTRY

Purpose: Customizes the time, date, and currency conventions to those of the desired country and language.

Syntax: COUNTRY = xxx (where xxx is a three digit country code)

Default: COUNTRY = 001

Environment: DOS Mode and OS/2 Mode

Remarks: Different countries have different ways of representing time, date, and currency values. You may set OS/2 to use the conventions of the country of your choice. The default country is the U.S.A. Table 8.2 lists the countries supported by OS/2, their corresponding country codes, associated default code pages, and default keyboard layouts.

Table 8.2
Countries Supported
by OS/2

Country	Country Code	Code Pages	Keyboard Layout
United States	001	437,850	US
Canada (French)	002	863,850	CF
Latin America	003	437,850	LA
Netherlands	031	437,850	NL
Belgium	032	437,850	BE
France	033	437,850	FR
Spain	034	437,850	SP
Italy	039	437,850	IT
Switzerland	041	437,850	SF,SG
United Kingdom	044	437,850	UK
Denmark	045	865,850	DK
Sweden	046	437,850	SV
Norway	047	865,850	NO
Germany	049	437,850	GR
Australia (English)	061	437,850	—
Japan	081	—	—
Korea	082	—	—
China (PRC)	086	—	—

continued

Table 8.2
Countries Supported
by OS/2 (continued)

Country	Country Code	Code Pages	Keyboard Layout
Taiwan	088	—	—
Asia (English)	099	437,850	—
Portugal	351	860,850	PO
Finland	358	437,850	SU
Arabic	785	437	—
Hebrew	972	437	—

Example: We can set the country to Norway and convert time, date, and currency to Norwegian conventions with the command,

```
COUNTRY = 047
```

DEVICE

Purpose: Specifies the addition of a device driver to OS/2.

Syntax: DEVICE = [drive:][path] filename [arguments]

Default: none

Environment: DOS Mode and OS/2 Mode

Remarks: This command specifies the path to a device driver to be added to OS/2 so that a nonstandard device may be used with the system. Device drivers are explained in detail in the next section.

Example: To install a Mouse Systems PC Mouse on the COM2 serial port of your system, usable in both real and protected modes, issue the following command:

```
DEVICE = mouseaOO.sys serial=COM2
mode=b
```

DEVINFO

Purpose: Prepares individual input and output devices for code page switching.

Syntax: DEVINFO = devtype,subtype,[path]filename,[ROM= [(]xxx[,yyy)]]

Default: none

Environment: DOS Mode and OS/2 Mode

Remarks: Provides OS/2 with an exact description of an I/O device that is affected by a code page switch. If no path information is given, OS/2 assumes that the code page table file is in the root directory of the boot drive.

Example: To set up an EGA screen for code page switches, you might use a command like the following:

```
DEVINFO = scr,ega,display.tbl
```

FCBS

Purpose: Sets the number of file control blocks that can be concurrently open.

Syntax: FCBS = x,y (where x is the number of files that OS/2 may open at one time via file control blocks, and y specifies the number of files opened by file control blocks that OS/2 cannot close automatically). Both x and y may range between 1 and 255. The value of x must be greater than or equal to the value of y.

Default: FCBS = 4,0

Environment: DOS Mode only

Remarks: Most applications are opened and closed through the use of file handles rather than file control blocks. Some older applications may require the use of file control blocks. Put an FCBS command in your "config.sys" file only if one of your applications requires it. Such applications can only be run in DOS mode.

Example: To open five files using file control blocks and to protect the first three from being closed, add the following line to your "config.sys" file:

```
FCBS = 5,3
```

IOPL

Purpose: The Input/Output Privilege Level determines whether or not an application (process) will have access to input/output devices.

Syntax: IOPL = yes
> or
> IOPL = no

Default: IOPL = no

Environment: DOS Mode and OS/2 Mode

Remarks: This command is to be used only if you have one or more applications that are linked with IOPL segments and that use I/O instructions. A value of "yes" means that input/output privilege is to be granted. A value of "no" means that no such privilege is granted.

Example: To run an application requiring I/O privilege, put the following command into your "config.sys" file:

```
IOPL = yes
```

LIBPATH

Purpose: Specifies the location of the library of dynamic link modules.

Syntax: LIBPATH = drive:pathname[;drive:pathname][. . .]

Default: The default location is the root directory of the boot drive.

Environment: DOS Mode and OS/2 Mode

Remarks: The LIBPATH command is similar to the OS/2 PATH command in that it specifies directories to be searched for certain files. In this case, those files are dynamic link libraries. However, with the LIBPATH command, only the directories specified are searched. The default or current directory is not searched. One LIBPATH command can specify the searching of several directories. The path specifications should be separated from each other with semicolons.

Example: If you put all your dynamic link libraries into a directory on your hard disk named "linklib", you could access those libraries with the command,

```
LIBPATH = C:\linklib
```

MAXWAIT

Purpose: Assures that low priority processes do not have to wait more than the specified period to receive some CPU time.

Syntax: MAXWAIT = x (where x is the maximum number of seconds that may elapse before a process receives a temporary boost in priority)

Default: MAXWAIT = 3

Environment: DOS Mode and OS/2 Mode

Remarks: The OS/2 scheduler decides which active applications will run and when. If an application has not been run for the number of seconds specified in the MAXWAIT command, that process is given a temporary boost in priority for one execution cycle or *timeslice*. Thus you can be sure that even the lowest priority process is getting at least one timeslice worth of processor time every x seconds.

Example: To assure that low priority processes are given a priority boost at least once every five seconds, include into your "config.sys" the command:

```
MAXWAIT = 5
```

MEMMAN

Purpose: Controls memory management options.

Syntax: MEMMAN = noswap,nomove
   or
   MEMMAN = swap,move
   or
   MEMMAN = noswap,move

Default: If boot disk is not a floppy, default is:
   MEMMAN = swap,move
   If boot disk is a floppy, default is:
   MEMMAN = noswap,move

Environment: DOS Mode and OS/2 Mode

Remarks: With the MEMMAN command, you can choose whether or not to use OS/2's two principal memory management techniques, *swapping* and *moving*. Swapping means temporarily copying information that is active but not being used at the present moment to the swap area on your hard disk. When it is needed, the information will be swapped back into system memory again. Moving is relocating data segments within system memory. Both of these techniques substantially improve system performance when more than one task is running.

   You can see from the syntax above that it is possible to move without swapping, but it is not possible to swap without moving. If swapping is enabled, then moving must be enabled also. Normally you would run with both swapping and moving enabled. Only if you are running a time-critical dedicated operation should you disable swapping and moving.

Example: If you are booting from a floppy disk but have a hard disk available, you should issue a MEMMAN command to enable swapping. Add the following command to your "config.sys" file:

```
MEMMAN = swap,move
```

PRIORITY

Purpose: Allows the operator to circumvent the priority assigned to processes.

Syntax: PRIORITY = absolute
or
PRIORITY = dynamic

Default: PRIORITY = dynamic

Environment: OS/2 Mode Only

Remarks: Priority is divided into three classes, time-critical, normal, and idle-time. Each of these classes is further divided into 32 levels. Each process running in the system is assigned one of these priority levels. Within the normal class, priorities may be adjusted. When priority assignment is dynamic, OS/2 decides which jobs will receive priority boosts, and thus execute sooner. When priority is absolute, processes in the normal priority class are served strictly on a first-come, first-served basis. Since first-come, first-served is rarely the most efficient basis upon which to assign priority, you may never want to use the following command:

```
PRIORITY = absolute
```

PROTECTONLY

Purpose: Selects the allowable mode(s) of operation.

Syntax: PROTECTONLY = yes
     or
     PROTECTONLY = no

Default: PROTECTONLY = no

Environment: DOS Mode and OS/2 Mode

Remarks: If you know that you will be running only OS/2 (protected) mode applications, you can improve the efficiency of OS/2 by telling it so with PROTECTONLY = yes. If you want to leave open the option of running a DOS mode application, you may leave the default setting in effect.

Example: To run only OS/2 mode applications, include in your "config.sys" file:
```
PROTECTONLY = yes
```

RMSIZE

Purpose: This command sets aside the specified amount of memory for DOS (real mode) applications.

Syntax: RMSIZE = x (where x is a positive integer between 0 and 640, representing memory allocation in kilobytes)

Default: The amount of memory set aside for DOS mode operation is total memory size minus the minimum amount required for OS/2 mode operation. If total memory is sufficient, the amount set aside for DOS mode operation is the amount of memory installed below one megabyte (either 512K or 640K).

Environment: DOS Mode and OS/2 Mode

Remarks: Since OS/2 itself uses a significant amount of the memory below the 640K level, if you have 1.5M or less, it is impractical to try to run a large DOS mode application concurrently with even one OS/2 mode session.

Since the RMSIZE command sets aside memory space for DOS mode operation, it only makes sense to use it in a system where PROTECTONLY = no. When PROTECTONLY = no, both DOS mode and OS/2 mode operations can be executed.

Example: If you know that the only DOS mode application that you will be running is a word processor that takes up no more than 128K, you could issue the following configuration command:

```
RMSIZE = 128
```

RUN

Purpose: Loads and starts execution of a program automatically at system initialization time.

Syntax: RUN = [drive:][path]filename[arguments]

Default: none

Environment: DOS Mode and OS/2 Mode

Remarks: If there are one or more applications that you always want to start every time you do a system initialization, specify them with RUN commands in the "config.sys" file.

Example: Suppose you have written a custom accounting application for a business. The computer in the accounting department should have this application running throughout the business day. Invoke it in the "config.sys" file with a RUN command as follows:

```
RUN = C:\account\mainacct.exe
```

SHELL

Purpose: Allows you to specify a DOS mode command processor other than the normal "command.com" processor.

Syntax: SHELL = [drive:][path]filename[arguments]

Default: SHELL = command.com

Environment: DOS Mode only

Remarks: This command is only used by system programmers who write their own DOS mode command processor instead of using the standard "command.com." Naturally, this command only comes into effect if PROTECTONLY = no.

Example: If a system programmer had written a new command processor named "topsyst.com" and placed it in subdirectory "\OS2", you could invoke it by placing the following command into your "config.sys" file:

```
SHELL = \OS2\topsyst.com
```

SWAPPATH

Purpose: Specifies the area set aside on disk for temporary swap file storage.

Syntax: SWAPPATH = drive:[path]

Default: SWAPPATH = C:\

Environment: DOS Mode and OS/2 Mode

Remarks: For the SWAPPATH command to have any effect, the MEMMAN command must allow swapping. It is wise to set up a separate directory on your hard disk for the swap file. You should not leave the default swap path in effect. The root directory of your primary hard disk (C:), should not be cluttered up with temporary swapped information.

Even worse than leaving the swap file in the root directory of your primary hard disk is putting the swap file on a floppy. Because of the low performance of the floppy, system operation will slow to a crawl when swapped information must be retrieved from it.

Example: The best place for the swap file is in a separate partition on your hard disk. If you have created such a partition and named it "D:", you can activate it by putting the following command into your "config.sys" file:

```
SWAPPATH = D:\
```

TIMESLICE

Purpose: Specifies the minimum and the maximum amount of time that OS/2 will spend executing one process before it changes to the next process.

Syntax: TIMESLICE = x[,y] (where x is the minimum timeslice in milliseconds and y is the maximum timeslice in milliseconds)

Default: Set by OS/2

Environment: DOS Mode and OS/2 Mode

Remarks: The minimum timeslice must be greater than 31 milliseconds, and the maximum must be equal to or greater than the minimum. If only one number is specified, it is used for both minimum and maximum. Normally, the determination of the length of the timeslice should be left up to OS/2. Only if an application requires a specific timeslice value to run properly should you change the timeslice value.

Example: If you are running an application which works best when timeslice is set to 90 milliseconds, put the following command into your "config.sys" file:

```
TIMESLICE = 90
```

THREADS

Purpose: Sets the maximum number of threads that can be active at one time.

Syntax: THREADS = x (where x is a positive integer between 48 and 255)

Default: THREADS = 48

Environment: DOS Mode and OS/2 Mode

Remarks: The thread is the basic scheduling unit. An OS/2 system may run one or more concurrent sessions, each with one or more concurrent processes. Each process may consist of one or more threads. The default value of threads is the minimum number of 48. If you need more because you have a large number of activities occurring simultaneously, use the THREADS command to allow more threads to exist.

Example: You are running a combination of applications that require as many as 64 threads. Issue the following command:

    THREADS = 64

DEVICE DRIVERS

We have seen that one of the commands permitted in a "config.sys" file is the DEVICE command, which allows installation of a device driver. What are device drivers, and why do we need them?

A computer is useful only if we can get information into and out of it. OS/2 must control the passing of information between the computer's central processing unit (CPU) and the various input/output devices attached to it. Since the characteristics of these devices vary over a wide range, and since the designers of OS/2 cannot anticipate the requirements of I/O devices that have not yet been built, it makes sense to design OS/2 to have a common interface to all I/O devices.

Device drivers are programs that form the link between the common system interface and all the different I/O devices. Actually, there are two types of device drivers, character-oriented and block-oriented. Character-oriented device drivers handle data one character at a time. Examples of character-oriented devices are video screens and printers. Block-oriented device drivers handle data in blocks or groups of characters. Disk drives are examples of block-oriented devices. One block-oriented device driver can handle multiple devices.

Each different I/O device used by an OS/2 system must have a corresponding device driver. The device driver is a custom program written for the specific device with which it interfaces. Whenever a peripheral manufacturer markets a new I/O device, an appropriate device driver must be supplied with it.

The device drivers for standard devices, such as the keyboard, video display, parallel printer, floppy disk drive, hard disk drive, and RS-232 serial port are already incorporated into OS/2. Nonstandard devices must use *installable device drivers*. It is these installable device drivers that must appear in the "config.sys" file.

At boot time, the "config.sys" file is read and the system is configured. Part of this configuration is the inclusion into OS/2 of the device driver files mentioned in DEVICE statements. Once these device drivers become integrated into the operating system, you can begin using the associated devices.

OS/2 device drivers differ from DOS device drivers in that they must support both real and protected mode operation, and they must also support multitasking. In a single-tasking operating system such as DOS, a device driver could communicate with a slow device like a printer and wait for it to respond. Nothing else was going to happen until the I/O was complete anyway. However, in a multitasking system, you cannot afford the luxury of a device driver that keeps control until an I/O operation is complete. Instead, it must surrender control to the CPU so another task may execute while it is waiting for its I/O device to respond.

BUILDING AN EXAMPLE CONFIGURATION FILE

To illustrate the use of a configuration file, let's make some assumptions about the system you are using and the types of applications you are running. We assume that you are running an 80286 system with at least 2M of system memory and a single hard disk that has been partitioned as two logical devices. You have set aside a partition designated "D:" on your hard disk for the temporary swap file used to provide virtual memory capability. We will assume that you are running production programs that are thoroughly debugged.

Since the applications you are running are reliable, there is no need to invoke the BREAK command. The first command we will include in our example "config.sys" is BUFFERS = 30 because the default number of buffers (3) is grossly inadequate for a hard disk based system.

Assuming we are operating in the United States, the default settings of CODETABLE, COUNTRY, and DEVINFO are satisfactory. We need not include those commands in our example configuration file.

In addition to the standard input and output devices, we wish to use the PC Mouse from Mouse Systems. This requires an installable device driver specified by the DEVICE command. It takes the form

```
DEVICE = mousea00.sys serial=COM2
   mode=b
```

In the command we have chosen to attach the mouse to the serial port identified as COM2. We have also specified that the mouse may be used in both real and protected mode.

For our applications, the default settings of the FCBS, IOPL, LIBPATH, MAXWAIT, MEMMAN, PRIORITY, PROTECTONLY, SHELL, TIMESLICE and THREADS commands are fine. Therefore, these commands do not need to be included in our example file.

We want to set aside only enough space for real mode operation to contain a small word processor. The rest can be used for protected mode operation. The command,

```
RMSIZE = 128
```

will do the job.

To automatically commence execution of our main accounting application every time the system is booted or initialized we will include a RUN command,

```
RUN = C:\account\mainacct.exe
```

It specifies the location and the name of the application program.

Since we have set aside partition "D:" for the swap file, we must inform OS/2 with a SWAPPATH command,

```
SWAPPATH = D:\
```

Thus, the complete "config.sys" file is:

```
BUFFERS = 30
DEVICE = mousea00.sys,serial=COM2,
  mode=b
RMSIZE = 128
RUN = C:\account\mainacct.exe
SWAPPATH = D:\
```

EXERCISES

1. Construct a "config.sys" file for a system just like the one described above, but located in Denmark.

2. Build a "config.sys" file for a system whose largest real mode application requires 512K of memory.

3. Write a "config.sys" file for a system that has no hard disk and for which swapping is disabled.

SUMMARY

We have seen from the number and the complexity of the commands that may be included in the system configuration file that system configuration is an important matter which must be thoroughly understood to assure that your OS/2 system is delivering maximum performance. Although the default values for the configuration commands are adequate in many cases, in others they are not. When you first set up your system, take the time to consider the nature of the applications you will be running. Set the system configuration parameters accordingly by writing a customized "config.sys" file that is tailored to your specific needs.

Chapter 9

Batch Processing

WHAT ARE BATCH FILES?

Batch files, also known as *command files*, are *batches* of OS/2 commands that are executed as a group. Normally, when an OS/2 command is issued from the terminal, control is returned to the terminal after execution of the command is complete. However, when a command within a batch file is executed, control is turned over to the next command in the file rather than to the terminal. The terminal does not regain control until the entire batch file has been executed.

Batch file processing is more powerful under OS/2 than it is under DOS. There are two reasons for this. First, OS/2 has new commands that are not available under DOS. Second, some OS/2 commands that correspond to DOS commands of the same name contain additional features not present in the DOS versions.

DOS mode batch files always have an extension of ".bat". OS/2 mode batch files always have an extension of ".cmd". When you specify a batch file for execution, it is not necessary to include the extension. However, when in OS/2 mode, OS/2 will not execute a file with a ".bat" extension. Conversely, in DOS mode, OS/2 will not execute a file with a ".cmd" extension.

When a command is entered without an extension, OS/2 checks first to see if such an extensionless command exists. If so, it will execute the command. If not, OS/2 will look for a command with that name and the extension ".com". Next it will look for the command with the extension ".exe", then either ".bat" or ".cmd", depending on whether the current operating mode is DOS or OS/2. As soon as OS/2 finds a match, it will execute that program. For this reason, it is important to exercise some care when naming batch files. Be sure not to use a name that is already taken by a program file. When you think you are calling for the execution of your batch file, the program file of the same name will be executed instead.

BATCH SUBCOMMANDS

A batch file may contain normal OS/2 commands. In addition, it may contain special commands known as *batch subcommands*, which function only within batch files. There are eleven batch subcommands, each of which is described briefly here. Figure 9.1 shows a schematic representation of a batch file. It is a series of commands, listed one after another.

CALL

This command allows you to call one batch file from another, a process known as *nesting*. The process is analogous to calling a

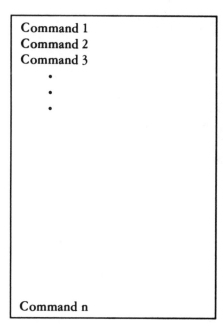

```
Command 1
Command 2
Command 3
    •
    •
    •




Command n
```

Figure 9.1
Schematic
Representation
of a Batch File

subroutine from a main program. When a CALL command appears within a batch file, execution of a second batch file is commenced. When execution of the second batch file is completed, control returns to the first batch file. Normally, execution commences at the statement following the CALL command. However, you may specify an argument with the CALL command that returns control to a different place in the first batch file. This capability does not exist in DOS.

Suppose you have a batch file named "batch1.bat", which contains the statement "CALL batch2". Further, suppose that "batch2.bat" contains the statement "CALL batch3". This is an example of batch file processing with two levels of nesting. Figure 9.2 shows what the flow of execution would be.

The subroutining ability provided by the CALL command lets you develop a library of batch files that perform frequently needed tasks. Selected batch files from the library can be invoked whenever needed merely by calling them from whatever batch file you are currently writing.

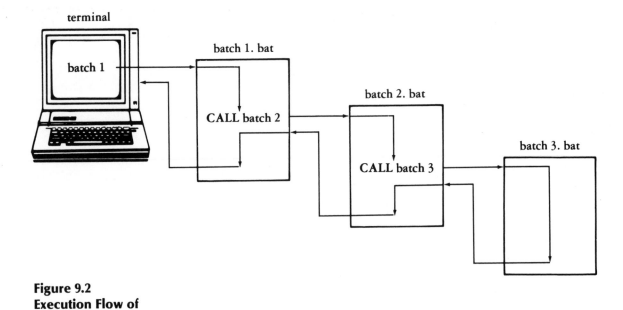

Figure 9.2
Execution Flow of
Nested Batch Files

ECHO

When batch files are run, you can follow the progress of the program because each batch command is displayed on the screen as it is executed. This display is due to the *echo* feature of OS/2. You can control whether or not batch commands are echoed to the screen with the ECHO command.

When you place an ECHO ON command in a batch file, all subsequent commands in the file are echoed to the screen. If the echo feature is on and you want to turn it off, use the ECHO OFF command. Subsequent commands in the file will not be echoed to the screen. A third form of the ECHO command is "ECHO [message]". You would typically use this form when *echo* is off to display a message on the screen.

Suppose you want to execute a batch file without the operator seeing any of the batch commands on the screen. If the first command in the file is "ECHO OFF," none of the following commands would be displayed. Only their effects would be evident. However, the first command in the file, "ECHO OFF" itself, would be displayed. OS/2 provides a method that is independent of the ECHO command to suppress the display of any batch command. By placing the "@" sign at the beginning of any batch command, the display of that command will be suppressed, regardless of the state of the ECHO switch. Thus to create a batch file that is not displayed during execution, make sure the first statement in the file is "@ECHO OFF". The following batch file displays a message without displaying any of the batch file itself:

```
@ECHO OFF
ECHO This message was created by a batch file.
ECHO Messages several lines in length may be
ECHO displayed in this manner.
```

The display created by this file would look like:

```
This message was created by a batch file.
Messages several lines in length may be
displayed in this manner.
```

The final form of the ECHO command has no argument whatsoever. When the ECHO command is entered without an argument, OS/2 responds by displaying the current state of the echo switch (ON or OFF).

ENDLOCAL

The ENDLOCAL command is used in conjunction with the SETLOCAL command to allow the batch file to have its own local drive, directory, and environment settings. With the SETLOCAL command, you can set up a path and environment that apply only to the current batch file. Use the ENDLOCAL command to restore the original system drive, directory, and environment settings.

Normally, the SETLOCAL and ENDLOCAL commands will occur in pairs, with some number of batch file commands between them. However, if you neglect to place an ENDLOCAL command after a SETLOCAL command, OS/2 will not generate an error message. It will merely restore your original environment settings after execution of the current batch file is completed. Since OS/2 can only handle one set of local environment variables at a time, SETLOCAL commands may not be nested.

EXTPROC

This command allows you to invoke an external command processor instead of using the normal "cmd.exe" in OS/2 mode or "command.com" in DOS mode. The external batch command processor that you specified will be in control while the batch file is executing. When the execution of the batch file is complete, control reverts to the original command processor.

To be valid, the EXTPROC command must be the first command in the batch file. Control is transferred to the external batch processor before any additional batch commands are executed.

FOR

The FOR command allows you to perform an OS/2 command on multiple items with multiple specifications in a single line. The FOR command works by binding a variable to the set of files specified, then invoking the OS/2 command in conjunction with the variable.

The syntax of the FOR command is as follows:

```
FOR %%c IN (item[. . .]) DO "command"
```

where "c" is any single character variable other than the numerals 0 through 9. The items may be files or paths. The percent sign must be doubled (%%) so that the batch file will interpret it as an operator and not as a character.

Suppose you have a number of backup files, all with the extension ".bak", scattered through three directories named "\memo," "\letter," and "\report." To free up some disk space, you now want to delete all those backup files. By using the FOR command, you can delete all those files with a single line in a batch file. The syntax would be:

```
FOR %%v IN (\memo\*.bak \letter\*.bak \report\*.bak) DO DEL %%v
```

This single command has the same effect as the following three OS/2 commands:

```
DEL \memo\*.bak
DEL \letter\*.bak
DEL \report\*.bak
```

In this case not much typing is saved, if any. However, there may be occasions where it will be useful to you to use one FOR command rather than multiple OS/2 commands.

If you would like to use a FOR command at the terminal rather than in a batch file, you may do so, but the syntax is slightly different. When the FOR command is typed in from the terminal, you do not have to double the percent sign. Since the batch file processor is not there to strip off a percent sign, only one should be used, as shown here:

```
FOR %c IN (item[. . .]) DO "command"
```

GOTO

The GOTO command is an unconditional branch command. It transfers execution from one point in the batch file to another point in the same batch file. The GOTO command allows you to bypass a group of batch commands and commence execution beyond them. It can also be used to loop back closer to the beginning of the batch file, but that is usually not a good idea. In order for program code to be understandable and maintainable, the use of the GOTO command should be held to a minimum. In particular, looping backward should be avoided.

IF

The IF command is used to evaluate the truth or falsity of a condition. When coupled with the GOTO command, the IF command gives OS/2 batch file programmers a conditional branch capability. The existence of the conditional branch function allows batch files to become quite sophisticated. One set of batch commands can be executed if a specified condition is true, and a different set of commands can be executed if the condition is not true.

Three types of conditions can be evaluated by the IF command.

1. If OS/2 has detected an error during the execution of the immediately preceding program, the fact that an error has been detected and the value of the error flag can be used to initiate an action (such as a program branch).

2. If one text string is identical to a second text string after parameter substitution, a specified action can be taken.

3. If a specified filename exists, an action can be taken.

Let's look at a few examples of the usage of the IF command. First, let's build a batch file that formats floppy disks. It is better to use such a batch file rather than using the FORMAT command directly because there is a danger that a typing error may cause you to accidentally format (and thus erase) your hard disk. A batch file that has already been written and proven to be correct does not carry this risk. Let's create a batch file named "flopform.cmd":

```
@ECHO OFF
FORMAT A: /s
IF errorlevel 0 GOTO FINISH
ECHO A formatting error has occurred.
:FINISH
REM End of batch file
```

We see from the @ sign and the ECHO OFF command that none of the batch commands are displayed on the screen. The FORMAT command performs the format operation on the diskette inserted into drive A. The IF command checks the error level. If it is zero (indicating no errors), execution branches to the end of the program. If the error level is non-zero (indicating that an error has occurred), execution does not branch, and the error message is displayed.

As a second example, suppose the batch file "compare.cmd" has been called from another program which has also passed it a parameter (%1). The calling command is "CALL compare %1". The parameter %1 represents a character string. You want to compare the character string represented by the parameter %1 to a reference string.

```
@ECHO OFF
IF %1 == Gold GOTO FIRST
IF %1 == Silver GOTO SECOND
IF %1 == Bronze GOTO THIRD
IF %1 == Finisher GOTO FINISH
ECHO You did not finish the race.
ECHO Better luck next time.
GOTO END
:FIRST
ECHO Congratulations! You finished
   first!
GOTO END
:SECOND
ECHO Congratulations! You finished
   second.
GOTO END
:THIRD
ECHO Congratulations. You finished
   third.
GOTO END
:FINISH
ECHO Congratulations. You finished.
:END
REM End of batch file
```

For our final example, let's consider a batch file whose execution depends on whether a certain file exists or not.

```
@ECHO OFF
IF NOT EXIST C:calc.exe COPY A:calc.exe C:
C:calc
REM End of batch file
```

If the program "calc.exe" exists, no action is taken at the IF statement, and the "calc" program is executed. If the program "calc.exe" does not exist on the hard disk, it is copied to the hard disk from the floppy disk installed in drive A. After being copied, the newly copied program is executed from the hard disk.

PAUSE

PAUSE is one of the simplest of the batch subcommands. All it does is suspend execution and display a message on the screen. You may specify a remark up to 121 characters long to be included in the message. Your remark line will not be displayed if ECHO is OFF.

After the optional remark, PAUSE displays the phrase, "Strike a key when ready . . .". Strike any key except Ctrl-C to resume execution.

If you terminate a PAUSE with Ctrl-C in OS/2 mode, the batch file is terminated, and control is returned to OS/2. If you terminate a PAUSE with Ctrl-C in DOS mode, OS/2 displays the message, "Terminate batch job (y/n)?" If you type "y", execution is terminated just as it is in OS/2 mode. If you type "n", execution of the batch file resumes where it left off.

PAUSE is useful for keeping messages on the screen long enough to be read and acted upon. It is often a good idea to place a PAUSE command immediately after a command that causes a screen display. When used with Ctrl-C, PAUSE is also a good way to enter breakpoints at intermediate stages in a batch file. Based on intermediate results, you may want to terminate execution of the batch file early. The PAUSE command/Ctrl-C combination provides a handy mechanism for such an early termination.

REM

If PAUSE is *one* of the simplest of the batch subcommands, then REM must be *the* simplest. It has no effect on the execution of the batch file at all. All the REM command does is display a remark on the screen. If ECHO is OFF, it doesn't even do that. Often REM statements are included in batch files that are intended to be run with ECHO OFF. They are there to remind the programmer of the function of the batch file or to explain the logic behind a sequence of commands. Here is an example batch file containing REM statements:

```
@ECHO OFF
REM  This remark is not displayed on the screen
REM  for the operator to see, but is here only
REM  for the benefit of the programmer who must
REM  maintain this code.
ECHO This remark is displayed on the screen for
ECHO the operator.
REM  End of this batch file.
```

SETLOCAL

This command allows you to define drive, directory, and environment variable settings that are local to the current batch file. After you have used these settings in your batch processing, you can restore the original system settings with an ENDLOCAL command. You may use multiple SETLOCAL commands within a single batch file, but you may not nest them. OS/2 will only keep track of the original system settings and one set of local settings at a time. If you do not include an ENDLOCAL command in your batch file to cancel the effect of the SETLOCAL command, your drive, directory, and environment variable settings will automatically revert to the original system values when you exit the current batch file.

As an example, suppose you are operating from your hard disk, but you want to perform a series of operations from the diskette in floppy drive A. You can create a batch file to perform those operations, and simplify the command syntax by setting the environment locally, as follows:

```
SETLOCAL
A:
PATH\
```

When you are finished, you may add an ENDLOCAL command if you wish. If you do not include an ENDLOCAL, control will revert to your hard disk and original path anyway as soon as execution of the current batch file is complete.

SHIFT

The SHIFT command manipulates the replaceable parameters associated with a batch file. If a string of replaceable parameters was specified when your batch file was called, the SHIFT command has the effect of discarding the leftmost parameter and shifting all the rest one position to the left. The following example illustrates how it works:

```
colors.cmd

:START
ECHO %1
SHIFT
IF %1 = " " GOTO :FINISH
GOTO START
:FINISH
```

Now if we execute the batch file (with ECHO OFF) and with the following parameters:

```
colors Red Orange Yellow Green Blue Purple Brown Black
```

the screen will echo the following sequence:

```
Red
Orange
Yellow
Green
Blue
```

```
Purple
Brown
Black
DOS1079: Syntax error: '==' unexpected.
```
As the SHIFT command causes the batch file to loop through the parameters one by one, at last there are no parameters left. At that point OS/2 issues an error message, since the "%1" replaceable parameter no longer refers to a real parameter.

CREATING BATCH FILES

Batch files are nothing more than ASCII files that have been created for a specific purpose. They can be created any way that ASCII files can be created. The two methods most commonly used to create batch files are text editors and the COPY command.

Using a Text Editor to Create Batch Files

Text editors (such as Edlin, which comes with OS/2) and word processors (such as WordStar, Word Perfect, and Microsoft Word) are all capable of creating batch files. When using a word processor, make sure that it is creating ASCII code rather than some other code. Specify that you want to create your file in nondocument mode.

The word processor or screen-oriented text editor of your choice is probably the best place for you to create batch files. You will be able to create the file, test it, and go back and change it if necessary. The larger the batch file, the more sense it makes to create it with a text editor.

Using the COPY Command to Create Batch Files

One problem with text editors and word processors is the time it takes to load them into memory and get them started. If you want to create a very short and simple batch file, it may be quicker to create the file directly from the OS/2 prompt with your terminal. One of the allowable ways to use the COPY command is to copy directly from the console device to a file on disk.

The major problem with this method of batch file creation is that once you have entered a line into the batch file you cannot go back and change it. If you find a small error in the batch file after testing it, you will have to reenter the entire file. This can be tedious if the batch file is more than three or four lines long.

So, to create any batch file longer than a few lines, use a text editor. For short ones, it makes sense to use the COPY command. Perhaps the best solution is to keep an OS/2 mode text editor application running as a process in your multiprocessor system.

When you need to create or modify a batch file, you can switch the text editor to the foreground and take the necessary action quickly and easily.

REPLACEABLE PARAMETERS

When we were discussing the SHIFT command, we mentioned replaceable parameters. A more thorough discussion of these useful devices is now in order.

With batch files, we can perform a variety of manipulations on various kinds of data. When writing the batch file, we may not know exactly what data will be manipulated, but we do know the general characteristics of the data. It is possible to write a useful batch file even though we do not know what data it will be used with. The identity of the data can be supplied just before the batch file is executed. In fact, one batch file may be used many times to perform the same operation on several entirely different sets of data.

Here is a very simple example of a batch file that makes use of a replaceable parameter. This batch file searches a directory for a specific text file and displays it on the screen if it is present.

```
jackpot.cmd

ECHO OFF
CHDIR %1
IF EXIST %2 GOTO :OUTPUT
ECHO No jackpot this time.
GOTO :END
:OUTPUT
TYPE %2
:END
```

You might invoke "jackpot.cmd" as follows:

```
jackpot direct1 winner.txt
```

OS/2 will search the directory named "\direct1" for a file named "winner.txt". If it finds the file in the designated directory, it will display the text of the file on the screen. If OS/2 does not find the file in the indicated directory, it will display the consolation message, "No jackpot this time."

TEMPORARY FILES

In the course of processing some batch files, you may need to create one or more temporary files to hold intermediate results. This could present a problem in a multitasking system if you are running the same batch file in more than one process at a time. If both batch files use the same temporary file, they could mix their data, providing erroneous results to both tasks.

One way to overcome this problem is to use replaceable parameters for filenames in the batch files. In this case, you can specify the temporary filenames at runtime and assure that there is no conflict with other processes. At the end of each task, it is wise to delete any temporary files that you have created. In that way your disk does not become cluttered with obsolete temporary files.

NAMED PARAMETERS

Named parameters, available in OS/2 mode only, are similar to replaceable parameters but are different in several important respects. First of all, you can give them meaningful names rather than the two character symbols for the ten replaceable parameters (%0-%9). A named parameter can be from one to six characters, delimited front and back by percent signs. Secondly, the values of named parameters are not specified at runtime. Rather, they are environment variables set by the SET command. You can set them within the batch file in which they are used, or you can set them before the batch file runs.

Although named parameters are used in much the same way as replaceable parameters, they have a few advantages. First, there is no restriction on the number of named parameters that you may have whereas a maximum of ten replaceable parameters may be used at one time. In addition, when using named parameters, there is no need to put so much information on the batch file's command line. Parameters may be set either beforehand or after the batch file has commenced executing.

As an example, let's construct a batch file that copies all files with an extension of ".exe" from one directory to another and then deletes them from the original directory. The batch file, named "cmdmov.cmd", would be:

```
@ECHO OFF
ECHO Verify that the source directory has been
ECHO specified with a "SET source=directory"
ECHO command, and the destination directory has
ECHO been specified with a "SET dest=directory"
ECHO command. If so, press any key. If not,
ECHO press Ctrl-C.
PAUSE
COPY %source%*.exe %dest%
IF NOT errorlevel 0 GOTO :FAULT
DEL %source%*.exe
ECHO Command files successfully moved.
```

```
GOTO :END
:FAULT
ECHO Command file move not completed.
:END
```

To use this batch file properly, you might use the following series of
commands:

```
SET source=\wordproc
SET dest=\cmdfiles
CMDMOV
```

THE "autoexec.bat" BATCH FILE

Perhaps the most important batch file of all is the one that sets up
your system for you when you first turn your computer on and boot
up. It can set the operating environment to all your preferred defaults
and even commence execution of your most commonly used application. In DOS mode, the batch file that can do all these things for you
is called "autoexec.bat". When the system boots up in DOS mode, the
first thing OS/2 does after the bootup is complete is look for a file
named "autoexec.bat" in the root directory. If OS/2 finds such a file, it
executes it. In your "autoexec" file, you can set paths to the directories
you normally use and set aside buffers to facilitate data transfer
between your CPU and the hard disk. You can also do anything else
that batch files are capable of doing to tailor the operating environment to meet your needs.

An example "autoexec.bat" might look like this:

```
ECHO OFF
BUFFERS = 30
SET path = C:\; C:\os2; C:\wordproc
PROMPT [Real $P]
CHDIR \wordproc
WS
```

This simple batch file establishes enough buffers to support your
hard disk and sets paths to the root directory, the directory containing
OS/2 system files, and the directory holding your primary application.
The PROMPT command changes the system prompt to indicate that
you are in DOS mode and to display the current drive and directory.
With CHDIR, you change the current directory to the one that
contains your word processing application, and with the "ws"
command, you start the word processor (in this case WordStar).

THE "startup.cmd" BATCH FILE

The "startup.cmd" batch file performs the same function in OS/2 mode that the "autoexec.bat" file performs in DOS mode. It customizes the system to your preferred operating environment. If you include a command to start up an application from this OS/2 mode batch file, you must make sure that it is an OS/2 mode application.

EXERCISES

1. Create a batch file named "batch1.cmd" that displays a directory of the root directory of your hard disk without displaying any of the commands of the batch file itself.

2. Make a subdirectory of the root directory named "subdir1". Next create a batch file named "batch2.cmd" that calls the batch file "batch1.cmd" as a subroutine, then displays the message, "Contents of the root directory." on the screen.

3. Create a batch file named "batch3.cmd" that deletes "batch2.cmd" if and only if it exists. Verify the correctness of "batch3.cmd" by checking for the existence of "batch2.cmd" before and after executing "batch3.cmd." After "batch2.cmd" has been deleted, run "batch3.cmd" again and verify that no error message is displayed for trying to delete a nonexistent file.

SUMMARY

Batch files can be powerful tools for manipulating files in both the DOS and OS/2 modes of OS/2. The batch subcommands provided by OS/2, when combined with normal OS/2 commands (which may also appear in batch files), can be used to perform any needed operation or combination of operations on the OS/2 system environment or on files stored on disk.

The ability to call one batch file from another and the ability to pass parameters from one batch file to another allow quite sophisticated programming to be done.

The "autoexec.bat" and "startup.cmd" batch files are arguably the most important of all batch files since you will use one of them every time you use your computer. The main purpose of these two files is the same as the main purpose of all batch files, to save you from repetitious data entry. Once you have frozen a sequence of commands into a batch file, you can invoke the entire sequence again by entering a single command line.

Chapter 10

Hard Disk Backup

FILE MANAGEMENT

OS/2 is a large software system. Programs and data files used with OS/2 tend to be large also. To store all this information, large capacity storage devices are necessary. At present, hard disk drives provide the best combination of speed and capacity for on-line data storage. Hard disk drives can provide storage for tens to hundreds of megabytes of information and make it available in milliseconds. All this capacity needs to be managed, however. If information were stored on the hard disk in a haphazard fashion, it would become progressively more difficult to find specific information when you needed it. To provide a structure for these large amounts of data, OS/2 offers the hierarchical directory system described in Chapter 5. By dividing the disk into subdirectories that contain only related files, it is possible to keep track of files easily. When any one subdirectory starts to contain too many files to be manageable, create several new subdirectories and parcel the files out among them.

By keeping related files together, it will be easier to know when a file is no longer needed and should be deleted. In many cases, all the files in a directory that contains an obsolete application should be deleted at the same time. All the files can be deleted with a single command (DEL *.*). After a directory has outlived its usefulness, you can remove it by changing to the root or parent directory and issuing a RMDIR command.

BACKING UP

Although there are occasions when you may want to erase data that is no longer needed, it is far more important that you are able to assure the safety of data that is still valuable to you. There are a number of misfortunes that might befall a hard disk that could cause it to lose the information you have stored on it.

First, there are commands that can be issued from the keyboard (such as FORMAT) that will destroy the information on your hard disk. If such a command is used incorrectly, accidentally, or maliciously, your data could be damaged or lost.

Other threats to your data must also be considered. A surge on the power line due to an electrical storm or power failure could irrecoverably scramble the data on your hard disk. The disk, along with your computer, could be physically damaged by fire, earthquake, tornado, or a host of other occurrences that are difficult or impossible to protect against.

The only way to be certain that you will not lose the valuable data that you have stored on your hard disk is to make duplicate copies of the data and store them somewhere else. That way, any disaster that destroys your primary data files will probably not destroy your duplicates too. This process of duplicating valuable information is called *backing up*. The duplicate files created are called *backup files*.

The Importance of Backup

Many people are lulled into a false sense of security by the high reliability of the modern hard disk. These devices carry mean time between failure (MTBF) ratings of from 20,000 to 50,000 hours. Based on these figures, if you were to run your hard disk for eight hours a day, five days a week, you could expect a failure after an elapsed period of between 9.6 and 24 years. However, these MTBF figures only relate to internally caused failures of the hard disk mechanisms themselves. The real threats to your data are operator errors and external problems such as power failures. These types of problems occur too frequently to ignore. You must protect your data against them.

Provisions for Backup in OS/2

OS/2 contains three commands that can be used to transfer data from a hard disk to another storage device. We have already encountered one of them, the COPY command, in a couple of other contexts. We introduce the second command, BACKUP, here since its only function is to transfer information from a hard disk to a backup device. The third command, XCOPY, is similar to COPY but also has several of the best features of the BACKUP command, including the ability to copy the subdirectories of the directory specified in the command. The primary mode of backup supported by these OS/2 commands is to transfer files from your hard disk to one or more floppy disks. These same commands will work just as well copying the contents of one hard disk to another hard disk. First, let's look at backing up to floppy diskettes.

Backing Up a Hard Disk to Floppy Diskettes

The floppy diskette is a convenient backup device for OS/2 systems because any computer running OS/2 that has a hard disk on it will also have at least one floppy disk drive. The floppy disk drive may be 3.5 or 5.25 inches wide. It may have a capacity of 1.44Mb, 1.2Mb, or even 360K. These differences in size and capacity are not important to the backup operation. Size has no effect. The only effect capacity has is in determining the number of diskettes that will be needed to complete the backup job.

Using COPY to Back Up a Hard Disk

The COPY command is not well suited to copying the entire contents of a hard disk to diskettes. For one thing, no file larger than the capacity of a single diskette may be copied. For another, you cannot copy a group of files that collectively exceed the size of a single diskette. You must divide up your files into groups, each of which takes up less space than a single diskette can hold. Each group must then be copied to a different diskette with a separate COPY command. This is a cumbersome procedure, and most people will not bother with it.

The COPY command is most useful when you are working on only a few moderately sized files each day. If you gather these files in a single subdirectory, it is relatively easy to copy them as a group to a backup diskette after you have finished your work for the day. For example, perhaps today you only worked on letters with your word processor. You could back up your letters with this single COPY command:

```
COPY C:\wordproc\letters\*.let A:
```

There are a few assumptions implicit in this command. One is that all your letters are contained in the "letters" subdirectory of the "wordproc" directory. Another assumption is that you flush out old letters fairly frequently, so that the subdirectory is not full of so many old letters that there are more than the backup floppy can hold. We are also assuming that all the files we wish to copy have an extension of ".let". Finally, we assume that the diskette installed in floppy drive A has enough free space on it to accommodate the letter files we are copying.

One advantage of using the COPY command for backup is that the files it creates on the backup floppy are identical to the original files on the hard disk. If we want to use these backup files at a later date, we need only insert the backup diskette into our system's floppy drive and access the needed file. It is immediately usable.

Using BACKUP to Back Up a Hard Disk

Unlike the COPY command, the BACKUP command was specifically designed to back up hard disks onto diskettes. It has some important features that specifically address the concerns of hard disk backup, and for that reason it is usually a better choice for backup than is COPY. A number of options are available, controlled by parameters. Parameters modify the operation of the BACKUP command. The syntax of the BACKUP command is as follows:

```
BACKUP [drive1:][path][filename]
    [drive2:] [/s][/m][/a] [/f]
    [/d:date] [/t:time] [/L:filename]
```

where "drive1" is the source drive that you want to back up and "drive2" is the destination drive to which the files will be backed up. The parameters are explained in Table 10.1 below.

Table 10.1
OS/2 BACKUP
Command Parameters

Parameter	Function
/s	Backs up all subdirectories of the directory specified by "[drive1:][path]"
/m	Backs up only those files that have changed since the last backup
/a	Appends files to an existing backup disk rather than overwriting any existing files on the destination disk, as is normally done
/f	If the destination diskette is unformatted and this switch is set, the diskette will be formatted before any attempt is made to transfer files to it; if the destination disk is a hard disk, this switch will *not* cause it to be formatted
/d:date	Backs up only those files modified on or after the specified date
/t:time	Backs up only those files modified at or after the specified time
/L:filename	Creates a backup log file named "filename" in the root directory; this file contains the date and time of the backup, the number of the backup disk, and the names of the files being backed up; if the backup log file already exists, the entries from the current backup operation are appended to it

If you wanted to back up all files in the "wordproc" directory of your hard disk and in all of its subdirectories that have been modified since January 1, 1988, you could use the following command:

    BACKUP C:\wordproc*.* A: /s /d:01-01-1988

NOTE: The format of the date may vary, depending upon which country code your computer is set for. See discussion of the DATE command in Chapter 12 and discussion of codepages for further information on national differences in date representations.

Using XCOPY to
Back Up a Hard Disk

XCOPY is a more sophisticated relative of the COPY command. It incorporates some of the same parameters as the BACKUP command plus some new ones that are unique to XCOPY. The syntax of XCOPY is as follows:

```
XCOPY [drive:][pathname1] [[drive:][pathname2]]
    [/s] [/e] [/p] [/v] [/a] [/m] [/d:mm-dd-yy]
```

The first set of drive and pathname specifications indicates the source, and the second set of drive and pathname specifications indicates the destination. Table 10.2 explains the parameters associated with the XCOPY command and their functions.

Table 10.2
OS/2 XCOPY
Command Parameters

Parameter	Function
/s	Copies all subdirectories along with the specified directory
/e	Used only in conjunction with the "/s" switch, the "/e" switch copies all empty subdirectories
/p	Prompts you with (Y/N)? to obtain confirmation for every file you have specified for copying
/v	Verifies every file copied is identical to its source file
/a	Copies only those specified files that have their archive bit set; does not modify the archive bit
/m	Acts like the "/a" switch but turns off the archive bit in the source file after the file has been copied
/d:mm-dd-yy	Copies only those files that were modified on or after the specified date; the date format may vary from that shown here depending on the country code you are using

As an example, let's say that you want to copy all files in the "\spread" directory (including all of its subdirectories) that have been modified since January 15, 1988 from hard disk to floppy. Issue the following command:

```
XCOPY C:\spread\*.* A:\spread\*.* /s /d:01-15-1988
```

If you rely on defaults for the destination pathname specification, the result will be somewhat different:

`XCOPY C:\spread\*.* A: /s /d:01-15-1988`

All files will be copied, as will all subdirectories, but the files in the "\spread" directory itself will be copied into the default directory on the destination drive, rather than into a directory named "\spread."

Backing Up One Hard Disk with Another

The three commands used to back up a hard disk to floppy diskettes, COPY, BACKUP, and XCOPY, can also be used to back up one hard disk to another. Let's examine when it makes sense to back up a hard disk with another hard disk.

First of all, backing up one hard disk with another one connected to the same system protects the data against some threats but not against others. A single operator error would probably not destroy the data on both disks. On the other hand, a power surge that knocked out one hard disk would probably destroy the other one too. Other threats like fire and earthquake will destroy two hard disks just as readily as one. Thus, backing up one hard disk with another probably only makes sense if the backup hard disk is a *removable media* hard disk. With such a system, after the backup is complete, you can remove the backup disk and transport it to a safe place.

A second consideration is, "Which of the three commands used for backup is the best to use when copying the contents of one hard disk to another hard disk?" If the backup hard disk has a capacity at least equal to the capacity of the primary hard disk, the biggest weakness of the COPY command is overcome. You do not need to worry whether the group of files you are copying will exceed the capacity of the backup disk. On the other hand, COPY will not automatically copy subdirectories, so it is not possible to copy an entire directory structure with a single command.

Although it will work, the BACKUP command is not well suited for backing up from hard disk to hard disk. Since the capacity of the backup disk is as great as the capacity of the primary disk, the fact that BACKUP allows a large file to be copied to a sequence of several destination disks is of no value. Furthermore, the fact that backed up files are not directly executable but must be restored back to another disk destroys much of the advantage of having your backup on a hard disk.

The best command to use when copying from one hard disk to another is XCOPY. Like COPY, it benefits from the fact that the destination disk is large enough to hold everything on the source disk.

The /s switch allows XCOPY to make a complete copy of the source disk, including all subdirectories. Finally, the backup copy can be executed directly. Since it is on a hard disk, the performance will be just as good as it was on the original source disk.

RESTORING BACKED UP DATA

The method of restoring backed up data will vary depending on which command was used to back it up in the first place.

Restoring Data Backed Up with the COPY Command

If hard disk data has been backed up to a series of floppy diskettes, it must be copied back to a hard disk to be used effectively. This is typically a straightforward procedure. You can use the same syntax that was used to create the backup copy in the first place, with the sole exception that the source and destination drive designations are reversed. Thus if you created a backup copy with the following command:

```
COPY C:*.* A:
```

you can copy it back from floppy to hard disk like this:

```
COPY A:*.* C:
```

Actually, it is not absolutely necessary that you restore data that has been copied to floppy. To use the data, merely insert your backup floppy into your floppy drive and access the data directly. In situations where you just need one quick access to a file that has been backed up with COPY, it may be easier to access the file from floppy than to copy it back to your hard disk and then access it from there.

Restoring Data Backed Up with the BACKUP Command

Data that has been backed up with the BACKUP command cannot be accessed directly from the backup floppy. The backup files have been changed into a form that is not executable. The only way to recover a file that has been copied with the BACKUP command is to copy it back to hard disk with the RESTORE command. The RESTORE command is the inverse of the BACKUP command. Either command is worthless without the other. RESTORE has the following syntax:

```
RESTORE drive1: [drive2:][pathname]
     [/s] [/p] [/b:date] [/a:date]
     [/e:time] [/l:time] [/m] [/n]
```

where "drive1" contains the backed up files and "drive2" is the destination drive. Pathname identifies the files to be restored. The parameters for RESTORE are defined in Table 10.3.

The options provided by the switches should allow you to easily specify which files on the backup disk should be restored and which should not. To restore all the files that we copied from the

Table 10.3
OS/2 RESTORE
Command Parameters

Parameter	Function
/s	Restores subdirectories as well as the specified directory
/p	Prompts for permission to restore a file over the top of an existing read-only file or a file that has been modified since the backup was made
/b:date	Restores only files that were modified on or before the specified date
/a:date	Restores only files that were modified on or after the specified date
/e:time	Restores only files that were modified at or earlier than the specified time
/l:time	Restores only files that were modified at or later than the specified time
/m	Restores only those files that were modified since the last backup
/n	Restores only those files that no longer exist on the destination disk

"\wordproc" directory and its subdirectories in the example given for the BACKUP command, the command would be:

```
RESTORE A: C:\wordproc\*.* /s
```

There is no need to specify the date switch, since the backup disk contains only those files that were modified on or after 01–01–1988, which are the files we want.

Restoring Data Backed Up with the XCOPY Command

As with the COPY command, to restore data that was backed up with XCOPY, you need to use another XCOPY command but with the source and destination disk designations reversed. To restore the spreadsheet files that were backed up to the "\spread" directory and its subdirectories in the earlier example of the use of the XCOPY command, merely use the same syntax, except for the drive designations. Thus, where the command used to perform the backup was:

```
XCOPY C:\spread\*.* A:\spread\*.* /s /d:01-15-1988
```

the command to restore all those files to the hard disk is:

```
XCOPY A:\spread\*.* C:\spread\*.* /s
```

Once again, we need not include the date parameter, since the only files on the backup disk are those that were modified on or after 01–15–88.

WHEN TO BACK UP

A backup is a form of insurance against data loss. It is only valuable if it is very close to being the same as the data on your hard disk at the time that you lost it. It stands to reason that if you are changing programs or data on a daily basis, you ought to back up daily too. If you back up daily, at most you will lose one day's work when your system crashes. If you back up weekly, you might lose as much as a week's work. That could be considerably more costly. If you do not back up at all and the data on your disk is critical to the conduct of your business, a disk failure could threaten your ability to remain in business.

If you follow a few simple guidelines, you will be well protected from data loss:

1. Back up all data that you cannot easily afford to lose, at the first opportunity.
2. Establish a habit of backing up at the same time of day, every day that you use your computer.
3. Make your backup procedure as simple as possible, so that you will not be tempted to skip it.
4. Maintain at least two independent sets of backup disks and alternate them. If you are backing up to one of them when your system fails, you will still be able to restore from the other.
5. Periodically transport backup copies to a site far removed from your system to protect against threats such as fire or flood.

If you follow these five simple rules, you will be well protected against all the major threats to your data.

UPGRADING YOUR HARD DISK TO A NEW VERSION OF OS/2

Since OS/2 is being released in phases with new features and capabilities becoming available every few months, you will probably want to upgrade to the latest version whenever a new one becomes available. The files you have created with the current version of OS/2 will continue to run without modification on all subsequent versions.

However, you may want to change them anyway to take advantage of new features that become available with the later versions.

When you acquire a new version or a new edition of OS/2, just follow the installation instructions that come with it. You will need additional hard disk space to hold the files associated with the new features, but your existing directory structure will continue to contain the bulk of the OS/2 system files.

RECOVERING DAMAGED FILES AND DISKS

There are a variety of problems that can cause the data on a hard disk to become irretrievable. A power surge experienced while the read/write head is writing to the disk could cause the information on the disk to become scrambled. This scrambling operation is called *creating bad sectors*. Bad sectors contain bit patterns that will be interpreted in an unpredictable way when they are read. If a critical area on disk goes bad, the entire disk may be rendered unreadable. In most cases the bad data is interpreted as a command which the computer attempts to execute. The result is usually a *system hang*, in which the computer no longer responds to keyboard input. You must shut the computer down completely and then turn it on again to regain control.

OS/2 provides a command, RECOVER, to retrieve as much data as possible from a disk that contains bad sectors. RECOVER can also be used to rescue a single file that contains one or more bad sectors. The syntax of the RECOVER command can take either of the following two forms:

    RECOVER drive:

or

    RECOVER [drive:][path]filename

The CHKDSK command will reveal whether your disk has any bad sectors or not. If it does, the RECOVER command may salvage some data for you that would otherwise be lost. RECOVER reads the specified file or disk, sector by sector, skipping over bad sectors wherever it finds them. Once it has skipped over a bad sector, OS/2 will no longer allocate data to that location.

There are a couple of situations in which the RECOVER command will not work. First, if you are using a remote workstation on a network, RECOVER will not work for you. Second, RECOVER will not function properly on a drive to which either the SUBST or JOIN command has been applied.

The RECOVER command should allow you to retrieve the bulk of the damaged file or disk. Only the sectors containing the bad spots will be lost. Hopefully you will be able to reconstruct that small amount of lost information more readily than you could reconstruct the entire disk.

SUMMARY

The large size of OS/2 itself and of the application programs it supports necessitates the use of high capacity storage devices. At the present time, hard disk drives are the best all-around high capacity storage devices available. Since use of a hard disk concentrates all of your valuable information in one place, failure of that one device could be devastating to your business. To assure that such a single point failure does not have disastrous consequences for you, it is vital that you back up your hard disk properly. An ongoing hard disk backup program is a form of insurance. You hope you will never need to use it, but if the need ever does arise, a good backup copy of your data can save you a tremendous amount of time and money.

This chapter discusses the commands provided by OS/2 that can be used to perform a hard disk backup operation. It also covers the restoration of backed up files to a new operational hard disk, should your original hard disk be damaged. Of course restoration is just as important as backup. The most religiously maintained backup procedure in the world is of no value if the backup files cannot be successfully reinstalled on a hard disk where they can be used. Options available with the BACKUP, RESTORE, and XCOPY commands give you considerable flexibility in deciding just which files to back up and which to restore.

Sometimes small localized regions on a hard disk become unreadable. If such a region happens to be located within one of your large, important files, the entire file may become inaccessible. To help you to rescue most of your data, OS/2 provides the RECOVER command. By using RECOVER, you can cut out the sector or sectors that contain the bad spot. The rest of your file becomes accessible again.

Chapter 11

Printing

INTRODUCTION

One of the primary ways of extracting information that is stored on a computer is to print the information out on paper. This printout can be in the form of an elaborate report, or it can be no more than an unformatted dumping of data. In a multitasking system such as OS/2, the system must assure that printed output from simultaneously running programs does not get intermixed. This segregation of printed output is achieved through a program called the *spooler*. In this chapter, we will describe how to generate printed output and also explain the operation of the spooler.

PRINT DEVICES

Application programs written in any of the available computer languages may generate printed output. This output can be directed to a variety of devices that produce *hardcopy*, which is another name for printed output. Such devices include all kinds of printers, including dot matrix, daisy wheel, laser, inkjet, as well as high speed line printers. Other hardcopy devices include plotters and screen-capture cameras. In addition to the printing capabilities of application programs, the OS/2 operating system itself provides several methods of printing out the contents of existing files. These methods typically work only with printers. Plotters and cameras require specialized software to function properly.

PRINTER PORTS

There are two standard kinds of input/output (I/O) ports that allow a computer running OS/2 to communicate with the outside world. They both are capable of transmitting information either into or out of the computer. In this discussion of printing, we are only concerned with the use of these ports for output of information to a print device. We will discuss each kind of port briefly.

The Parallel Printer Port

The parallel ports on machines that are running OS/2 are actually bidirectional ports, capable of transmitting information both into and out the computer. When such a port is attached to a printer, however, data flows in only one direction, from the computer to the printer.

The parallel port is called a parallel port because eight bits of information are sent out of the port in parallel. These eight data bits travel along eight parallel wires in the printer cable, and all arrive at the printer at the same time. The printer interprets these eight bits (also known as a byte) as a single ASCII character. ASCII is a standard form of encoded information that is understood and used by a wide variety of computers. Those ASCII characters that correspond to letters and numbers are printed out directly. Those characters that correspond to control codes are interpreted, then their function is executed. Examples of actions caused by control codes might be the starting of underlining, the ending of underlining, issuing a carriage return, etc.

Since each printed character or control code is represented by an eight-bit ASCII character, it is very efficient to send these characters to the printer in the form of an eight-bit byte, via a parallel port. Under OS/2, the first parallel port on the system is considered by default to be the primary printer port. You can change this default setting if you wish.

The Serial Printer Port

The serial port, also known as the asynchronous communications port, is just as capable of bidirectional communication as the parallel port is. However, once again, when it is attached to a printer, data flows only one way, from computer to printer. As the name implies, the serial port transmits each byte of information serially, one bit at a time. All data bits travel over the same wire in the serial printer cable, rather than each bit having its own wire as is the case with the parallel port.

As you might expect, it is possible to transmit information faster through a parallel port than is possible through a serial port. The serial port does have a compensating advantage, however, in that a serial printer may be placed much farther from the computer. Parallel printer cables will not work reliably if they are more than a few feet long. Serial cables as long as one hundred feet will still work well.

Setting Parallel Printer Modes with the MODE Command

The MODE command is used to set operating parameters for input and output devices. One of its uses is to specify parallel printer modes. When setting the parameters of a parallel printer, use the following syntax for the MODE command:

```
MODE LPTn[:][characters][,[lines][,p]]
```

The parameters have the following interpretation:

Parameter	Function
n	Specifies the number of the printer: 1, 2, or 3
characters	Specifies the number of characters per line, 80 or 132
lines	Specifies the vertical spacing, 6 or 8 lines per inch
p	Specifies that the computer will continue to try to send output to the printer, even if a timeout error has occurred

The default values for these parameters are LPT1, 80 characters per line, and 6 lines per inch. If the "p" parameter is set, you can break out of a timeout loop by pressing Ctrl-Break.

With this command, you can customize OS/2 to the specific characteristics of each of your printers. For example, let's say you have installed a wide-carriage printer on the second parallel port on your system. In order to have OS/2 send it information in the proper format, issue the following MODE command:

```
MODE LPT2: 132
```

Since you want to retain the default vertical spacing of 6 lines per inch, there is no need to specify the lines parameter in the MODE command.

Setting Serial Printer Modes with the MODE Command

Setting the operation parameters of the serial ports is somewhat more complex than it is for the parallel ports. There are more parameters to specify, as you can see from the following syntax line:

```
MODE COMm[:] baud[,parity[,databits
     [,stopbits][,p]]]
```

The parameters for this form of the MODE command are defined in Table 11.1.

To demonstrate the way a MODE command would be used with a serial printer, consider a laser printer with a serial interface capable of receiving data at a rate of 9600 baud. Since your modem is connected to the COM1 port, the printer is attached to COM2. You can get the computer and the printer talking to each other with the command:

```
MODE COM2: 96
```

Once again, you need not specify the parity, databits, and stopbits parameters, since the default values for them are correct.

Table 11.1
OS/2 MODE
Command Parameters

Parameter	Function
m	Specifies the number of the asynchronous communication (COM) port, which ranges from 1 to 8
baud	The first two digits of the serial transmission rate measured in baud: 110, 150, 300, 600, 1200, 2400, 4800, 9600, or 19,200
parity	Specifies parity: none (N), odd (O), or even (E); the default value is E
databits	Specifies the number of data bits per character, 7 or 8; the default value is 7
stopbits	Specifies the number of stop bits at the end of a character, either 1 or 2; if the baud rate is 110, then the default number of stop bits is 2; otherwise, the default number of stop bits is 1
p	Specifies that the computer will continue to try to send output to the printer, even if a timeout error has occurred

COMMANDS THAT PRINT

Although many applications provide print facilities of their own, OS/2 also provides us with several commands that can be used to output information to a printer. If you are working with an application that has its own print capability, by all means use it. However, if you are writing your own application or if the application you are running does not provide for printing, you may use the OS/2 commands. We will discuss each of these commands thoroughly enough for you to be able to use them.

The PRINT Command

PRINT is the command most often used with OS/2 to direct output to a printer. One convenient aspect of PRINT is that you can set up a print queue that contains all the files you want to print. Once the print operation has been set into motion, PRINT will print out all the files in the queue without any further operator intervention. Several options or *switches* are available as parameters with the PRINT command. Syntax is as follows:

```
PRINT [/d:device] [/t] [/c]
    [drive:][pathname] [...]
```

The parameters are defined below:

Parameter	Function
/d:device	Specifies the print device; the default device is LPT1; other possible devices are PRN, LPT2, LPT3, and COMm, where m = 1 to 8
/t	This parameter removes all remaining files from the print queue
/c	This parameter removes the immediately preceding filename, and all subsequent filenames from the print queue

Each entry in the print queue may have as many as 64 characters, including drive name and path specification. If your printer is connected to a serial port, be sure that the appropriate device driver for the port is installed. You cannot use an asynchronous port in OS/2 mode unless the device driver has been installed.

The COPY Command

We have already used the COPY command to copy files from one location on disk to another and to copy batch files from the console to a disk file. It can be used equally well to copy a file from disk or the console to a printer.

When we copy from the console to the printer, the result is much the same as it would be if we were typing into a typewriter. After we enter the first line, which might be

```
COPY con prn
```

every succeeding line will be printed out on the printer exactly as it is typed in. After the Enter key is pressed at the end of each line, that line will be printed out. When you are finished, merely enter Ctrl-Z to terminate the Copy process. The console will once again become usable for the entry of commands.

The TYPE Command

The TYPE command displays the contents of a text file on the screen. In DOS mode you can specify only one text file for display. In OS/2 mode, multiple test files can be displayed with a single TYPE command. DOS mode syntax is

```
TYPE [drive:][path]filename
```

In OS/2 mode, the command takes the following form:

```
TYPE [drive:][path]filename [...]
```

The ellipsis (...) represents additional file specifications.

We can use the TYPE command to output to the printer by redirecting output from the screen to the printer. The OS/2 mode syntax for such a redirected TYPE command would typically be:

```
TYPE [drive:][path]filename [...] >
   prn
```

The contents of the specified files would be printed on the primary printer rather than being displayed on the terminal screen. Say the default directory of the current disk includes a text file named "demo.txt" which contains the following data:

```
This is the first line of the demonstration file.
This is the second line.
```

To print this information out, enter the following command:

```
TYPE demo.txt > prn
```

The two lines of text given above would be printed out on the printer attached to the first parallel printer port.

THE SPOOLER

The spooler allows you to place a sequence of jobs in a print queue, then print them out in the background. Meanwhile, execution of multiple sessions in the foreground may be proceeding. The spooler controls the printing of output from multiple processes in such a way that concurrently running print operations do not interfere with each other.

The output of each active print job is sent to a temporary spool file on disk. When the entire print file has been copied to a spool file, it is added to the print queue. Each file in the queue is printed sequentially. In this way, all print jobs are printed in an orderly fashion. After a spool file has been printed, the temporary disk file is automatically erased.

When you perform the standard installation of IBM OS/2, the call to the spooler is automatically included in the startup code that is executed every time your system is booted. Thus, the default case is for the spooler to be active. If you wish to deactivate the spooler, you must remove the SPOOL command from the startup command file.

If you wish to send spooled output to two or more printers, you may execute a SPOOL command for each one. This will enable you to send certain types of print jobs to a dot matrix printer, for instance, and other jobs to a letter quality daisy wheel printer.

SUMMARY

Although most of the time you will be running applications that provide their own print facilities, occasionally you may want to print out text files without using an application. On those occasions, you can use the commands that OS/2 provides to generate printed output, the PRINT, COPY, and TYPE commands. You will need to know what kind of port your printer is attached to (parallel or serial), and you will want to make sure that the print mode of the computer is compatible with that of the printer. You will probably want to include the appropriate MODE command in your "autoexec.bat" file so that your printer is always properly configured, beginning at the very start of the workday.

The spool facility of OS/2 allows you to run several jobs simultaneously that all produce printed output. The printed output of each job is kept separate in a print queue, then printed, one job after the other, in the order in which they were completed.

Chapter 12

Command Reference

ABOUT OS/2 COMMANDS
REFERENCE SECTION

ABOUT OS/2 COMMANDS

There are two types of OS/2 commands, internal and external. The internal commands are part of OS/2 itself and are always present when OS/2 is active. The external commands reside on disk. OS/2 loads them into memory and executes them when they are invoked by the operator or by program. The installation procedure that you performed when you first put OS/2 on your system created directories to hold these command files and set the appropriate paths in the "os2init.cmd" and "autoexec.bat" batch files that are always executed whenever you restart your system.

Command lines may be up to 128 characters in length. This maximum applies to both DOS and to OS/2 mode.

If a command displays so much information that the information starts to scroll off the top of the screen, you can pause the display by pressing Ctrl-S. Resume display by pressing any key.

Commands may be entered in either upper or lower case, or a combination of the two. The command processor ignores case. Throughout this book, uppercase has been used exclusively, for the sake of clarity.

For some commands, the proper syntax in DOS mode is slightly different from what it is in OS/2 mode. In those cases, both syntaxes will be shown.

In the following pages, a detailed description of each command will be given. If the command being covered operates in DOS mode only, the [D] symbol will be placed at the top of the page. If the command operates in OS/2 mode only, the [O] symbol will be placed at the top of the page. No symbol will be placed at the top of the page for commands that operate in both DOS and OS/2 modes.

Command syntax will be shown in the form of a *command diagram*. The diagram illustrates the various options that are available with each command. Every command diagram has a baseline, and every term that appears on the baseline must be in the command. Terms that appear below the baseline are optional. A right-pointing arrow at the end of a command diagram line means that the diagram is continued on the next line. When a command diagram line is terminated with a vertical line, the diagram is complete.

For internal commands, the first term of the command is always the command itself. The CLS (clear screen) command is shown in this example:

CLS——|

One of the simplest of all OS/2 commands, it has no parameters.

External commands reside on disk. If the required command is located in a directory other than the current directory, and the proper path has not been set, the command can be executed by specifying the drive and path before entering the command. The FDISK command, represented below, is an external command:

[O]

As the baseline shows, if the FDISK command is either in the current directory or the proper path has been set, only the command word itself need be entered. The symbol above the command diagram shows that this command can be used only in OS/2 mode.

If a command term or group of terms can be specified more than once, this fact is shown by enclosing the repeatable terms within a backward pointing arrow called a *return arrow*. The OS/2 mode version of the MKDIR command illustrates this feature:

[O]

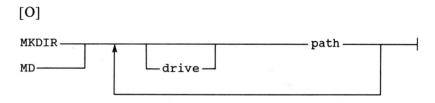

Either the MKDIR or MD form of the command may be used, and multiple directories can be created with a single command line merely by specifying each new directory's drive and path.

When parameters are shown stacked one below the other, this means that any one of the parameters in the stack may be chosen. This type of command can be illustrated with the ANSI command, which is diagrammed as follows:

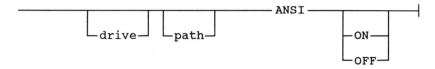

You may issue the ANSI command in any one of three ways: with no parameter, ON, or OFF.

When a stack of parameters is enclosed in a return arrow, it means that more than one parameter may be specified, and they may be specified in any order. Each parameter may be specified only once, however. The DOS mode version of the DIR command illustrates this type:

[D]

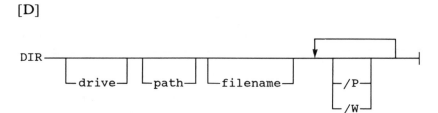

You can specify no parameter, the /P parameter, the /W parameter, or both /P and /W, in either order.

When a stack of parameters with no return arrow occurs within a stack of parameters that has a return arrow, only one parameter from the inner stack may be selected. This parameter may then be specified along with any of the parameters in the outer stack, again, in any order. One form of the PRINT command provides us with an example of this syntax:

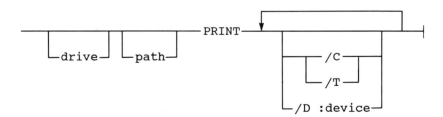

Either the /C or the /T parameter may be specified along with the /D parameter, but not both.

[O] ANSI

Purpose: Enables and disables support for extended display and keyboard features.

Syntax:

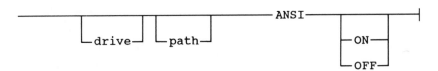

Parameters:

None	Displays the current setting (ON or OFF).
ON	Enables extended display and keyboard support.
OFF	Disables extended display and keyboard support.

Default: ON

Exit Codes: None

Remarks: Extended keyboard and display support allow you to redefine keys, manipulate the display cursor, and change the display color attributes. These manipulations of the keyboard and display are accomplished with *escape sequences*, which are sequences of control characters that begin with the Esc character. Some graphics programs may conflict with ANSI display control. Before running such a program, enter ANSI OFF. When you are finished with the graphics program, enable ANSI support again with the ANSI ON command.

Example: To disable extended keyboard and display support, enter

```
ANSI OFF
```

OS/2 will respond by executing the command, then reporting what it has done:

```
ANSI extended screen and
keyboard control is off.
```

Related Commands:
    DEVICE = ANSI.SYS in the config.sys file
    PROMPT

[D] APPEND

Purpose: Sets a search path for files outside the current directory that have extensions other than ".exe", ".com", and ".bat".

Syntax: The first time APPEND is loaded, it has the following syntax:

If you wish to specify the /E parameter, it must be done the first time APPEND is used after bootup or system reset. Although an external command, once APPEND has been loaded, it stays resident and behaves like an internal command on all subsequent invocations.

At any time during a DOS mode session, append may be used in the three following ways:

To specify directories to be searched:

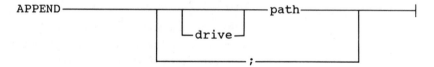

To remove the search path set by a previous APPEND or SET command:

```
APPEND—;————————————————————————————————————————————————————|
```

To display the search path set by a previous APPEND or SET command:

```
APPEND————————————————————————————————————————————————————————|
```

Parameters:

/E   When the /E parameter is specified the first time APPEND is used, paths specified by subsequent APPEND commands are kept in the DOS environment. This is similar to what is done with paths specified by the PATH command. Paths kept in the environment can be altered by SET commands as well as by APPEND commands.

Default: None

Exit Codes: None

Remarks: APPEND is very useful when you want to keep an application and its associated files in one directory while allowing it to access data in another directory.

Example: You have a word processing program, including overlay files and other auxiliary files in a directory named "\wordproc". Your document files are in other directories named "\memos", "\letters", "\reports", and "\articles". To write a letter, make the "\letters" directory the current directory, then issue the following commands:

```
APPEND \wordproc
PATH \wordproc
```

This will enable you to access all the files you need, both command files and others. Since the "\letters" directory is the current directory, any new versions of the letters you work on will be stored where they belong, in the "\letters" directory.

Related Commands:
PATH
DPATH
SET

[D] ASSIGN

Purpose: Directs the DOS mode processor to redirect all references from a specified disk drive to a different disk drive.

Syntax:

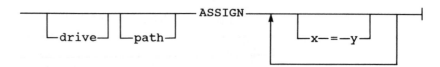

Parameters:

None   Resets all drives back to their original settings. This parameter only makes sense if a previous ASSIGN command has changed a drive assignment.

x   The single-character drive letter to which reads and writes are currently sent. Do not type a colon after the drive letter.

y   The single-character drive letter to which you want the reads and writes to be sent. Do not type a colon after the drive letter.

Defaults:

None   The default drive assignment is that no reassignment has taken place.

Exit Codes: None

Remarks: This command is useful if the application you are running assumes that you are using one disk drive, when in fact you are using another. Before hard disks became widespread, many applications assumed that only drive A and drive B (the floppy drives) were being used. Since you are using drive C and may not even have a drive B on your system, you will need to use the ASSIGN command to use this software.

Two commands, FORMAT and DISKCOPY, ignore the reassignments made by the ASSIGN command. This is done to protect you. Reassigning these two commands would serve no purpose and could be disastrous to your data. For example, if you were to issue the ASSIGN A=C command to run an application and then forget to revoke the assignment with another ASSIGN command with no parameters, your system would be a time bomb waiting to go off. At a later time, when you attempt to format a floppy disk with the

FORMAT A: command, you would format your hard disk instead. All those megabytes of data on your hard disk would be lost. Happily, the operating system protects you from this potential problem by causing FORMAT and DISKCOPY to ignore drive reassignments.

Examples: I made good use of the ASSIGN command when I switched operations from a PC to a PS/2 Model 50. The DOS mode software that I wanted to install on my Model 50 hard disk was all on 5.25-inch format diskettes. Of course the A drive on the Model 50 is a 3.5-inch unit, as it is on all PS/2 models. To transport software onto my new computer, I installed an external 5.25-inch floppy disk drive, the Matchmaker™ from Dolphin Systems, Santa Ana, California. Functioning as drive B, the external drive worked marvelously as a medium of information transfer to my new system.

There was however, a small problem. Some applications assumed that they would be installed onto the hard drive from drive A. Since the 5.25-inch program diskettes would not fit into the 3.5-inch A drive, these applications would have to be copied from drive B to drive A, then installed onto drive C from there. To avoid this extra operation, I used the ASSIGN command as follows:

```
ASSIGN A=B
```

Thereafter, when the application installation program told OS/2 to look for files on drive A, OS/2 looked on drive B instead. The installations proceeded without a hitch.

As a second example, let's say that you want to run a software package that assumes your program files are on drive A and your data files are on drive B. For performance reasons, you want to run the entire application from drive C. Issue the following command:

```
ASSIGN A=C B=C
```

Now when you run your application (which you have previously copied to your hard disk), all references to either drive A or drive B will be redirected to drive C.

Related Commands:
    SUBST
    JOIN

ATTRIB

Purpose: Changes the read-only attribute and the archive bit for a file or group of files.

Syntax:

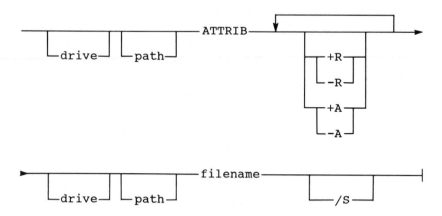

Parameters:

None	For the specified file or group of files, displays an "A" if the archive bit is set, and an "R" if the read-only attribute is ON.
+R	Turns on the read-only attribute for the specified file or group of files.
−R	Turns off the read-only attribute for the specified file or group of files.
+A	Turns on the archive bit for the specified file or group of files.
−A	Turns off the archive bit for the specified file or group of files.
/S	Processes all subdirectories of the specified directory.

Default: None

Exit Codes: None

Remarks: Whenever a file is created or modified, its archive bit is set ON. This bit may be used with the BACKUP, RESTORE, and XCOPY commands to selectively back up or copy those files that have been created or changed since the last backup or copy.

The read-only attribute allows you to keep a file from being changed or deleted. If you have important files that should never be changed or deleted, you can protect them from most operator-induced problems by setting their read-only attribute ON.

Examples: To turn off both the archive bit and the read-only attribute of a file in the root directory of your hard disk named "master.exe", use the following command:

```
ATTRIB C:\master.exe -R -A
```

To set the archive bit on for all text files on your hard disk use

```
ATTRIB C:\*.txt +A /S
```

All files with the extension ".txt" in the root directory and in all its subdirectories will have their archive bits set ON.

Related Commands:
BACKUP
RESTORE
XCOPY

BACKUP

Purpose: Backs up one or more files from one disk to another.

Syntax:

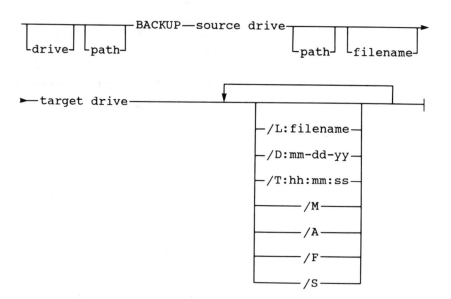

Parameters:

/L:filename   Creates or appends to the backup log named
        "filename". This file records the date, time, and
        the number of the backup disk containing each file
        backed up. This information can be used by the
        RESTORE command when you want to restore
        one file from a large collection of backup
        diskettes.

/D:mm-dd-yy   Backs up only those files that were created or
        changed on or after the date specified. The
        command processor expects the date to be in the
        proper format for the country specified with the
        COUNTRY command.

/T:hh:mm:ss   Backs up only those files that were created or
        changed at or after the specified time.

/M   Backs up only those files that have been modified
        since the last backup. In reality, it backs up only
        those files whose archive bit is set ON.

/A   Appends files to those already on the backup disk.
                If this parameter is not specified, all files on the
                backup disk will be erased before new backup files
                are copied to it.

/F   Causes the target diskette to be formatted before
                files are backed up to it. Do not use this
                parameter if you are backing up to a 360K
                diskette installed in a 1.2Mb drive. If the target
                drive is a hard disk, this parameter will not
                initiate a format operation.

/S   Causes the backup operation to extend to all
                qualifying files in all subdirectories of the
                specified directory.

Defaults: None

Exit Codes:

0   Normal completion (no error).

1   No files were found to back up.

2   Some files not backed up due to sharing conflicts.

3   Terminated by user.

4   Terminated due to error.

Remarks: If you are backing up a hard disk to floppies, be sure you
have enough blank floppies on hand to hold all the files you specify
for backup. If your backup floppies are not yet formatted, be sure to
specify the /F parameter to format them before files are copied to
them.

     If you are backing up one hard disk to another hard disk, be sure
there is enough room available on the target hard disk to hold all the
specified files.

     If your BACKUP command is embedded in a batch file, you can
use the exit codes to determine what to do next in the event that the
backup is not successfully concluded. The IF batch command checks
the *errorlevel* variable, which is set by the exit code.

Examples: A common use of this command is to back up an entire
hard disk to floppies. Do it with the following command:

     BACKUP C:*.* A:/S

As each floppy is filled, you will be prompted to remove it and to
insert another one.

     Another common practice is to keep a series of backups, each
one containing only those files that have been modified during the

preceding time period. Two backups made on consecutive Fridays would be done with the following commands:

```
BACKUP C:  A:/D:01-15-88
BACKUP C:  A:/D:01-22-88
```

If you make such a backup every Friday for a month, then do a complete backup such as the one given in the previous example, your data will be well protected. The weekly backups will not take long to complete since only a few files will have been modified since the last backup. The monthly backup will take longer, but after all, you only have to do it once a month.

Related Commands:
ATTRIB
IF (batch command)
RESTORE
XCOPY

[D] BREAK

Purpose: Enables or disables the checking for Ctrl-Break whenever a DOS mode application issues a system call.

Syntax:

Parameters:

None	Displays whether BREAK is currently ON or OFF.
ON	Enables the check for Ctrl-Break.
OFF	Disables the check for Ctrl-Break. When BREAK is OFF, OS/2 checks for Ctrl-Break only during standard input, output, print, and auxiliary operations.

Default:

OFF	If a value for BREAK is not specified in the "config.sys" file, the default value of BREAK is OFF.

Exit Codes: None

Remarks: If you are running a program that performs few input, output, print, or auxiliary operations (such as a compilation), you may want to set BREAK ON to give you a method of aborting execution before the application comes to its normal conclusion.

In OS/2 mode, the check for Ctrl-Break is always on. You cannot turn it off.

If you press Ctrl-Break while a DOS mode batch file is running, OS/2 will display the message,

`Terminate batch job (Y/N)?`

If you enter a "Y," the batch job will be terminated and you will be returned to the system prompt. If you enter "N," execution of the batch file will proceed. In OS/2 mode, you are not given this choice. When you press Ctrl-Break, you are returned immediately to the system prompt.

Examples: DOS mode operations are speeded up somewhat by reducing the number of times the operating system checks to see whether or not Ctrl-Break has been pressed. Instead of checking every time the running application makes a system call, a check will be made only when input or output operations are performed, if you issue the following command:

BREAK OFF

If you are debugging a new program that does not have much interaction with the keyboard or the screen, you may want to provide for an early termination by first entering,

BREAK ON

Related Command:

BREAK statement in "config.sys" file.

CHCP

Purpose: Displays the active code page number or allows you to switch to a new code page.

Syntax:

Parameters:

None   Causes the active code page number to be displayed.

nnn   Specifies the number of the new code page you want to start using.

Default: None

Exit Codes: None

Remarks: You can have two code pages prepared for your system at one time. Typically these would be your national language code page and the multilingual code page. The valid code pages are:

Page Number	Page Name
437	United States
850	Multilingual
860	Portuguese
863	French-Canadian
865	Nordic

The multilingual code page contains all the characters of most North American, South American, and European countries. It is an international data processing standard that is shared by IBM minicomputers and mainframes as well as by personal computers.

In order to successfully switch code pages, you must have certain statements in your "config.sys" file. These statements identify which two code pages are to be prepared for your system, and they also prepare the I/O devices accordingly.

Since the identity of the active code page affects what will be printed out on the printer as well as what is displayed on the screen, the print spooler must also be aware of what code page is active for each session that it is handling. The DEVINFO command in the "config.sys" file tells the spooler which code pages have been prepared.

Examples: To determine the identity of the active code page, enter
```
CHCP
```
OS/2 will respond with a message similar to the following one:
```
Active code page: 437
Prepared system code pages: 437 850
```
If provision for code page switching has not been set up in the "config.sys" file, the CHCP command will cause the following message:
```
No code page support is available on
  the system.
```
To switch from the current code page to the other one that has been prepared, issue a command like this one:
```
CHCP 850
```
To change back to the original code page, you must enter the appropriate version of the command:
```
CHCP 437
```

Related Commands:
    CODEPAGE in "config.sys"
    COUNTRY in "config.sys"
    DEVINFO in "config.sys"
    SPOOL

CHDIR

Purpose: Displays the name of the current directory or changes it to a new directory.

Syntax:

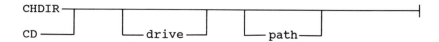

Arguments:

None   Displays the name of the current directory.

drive   This argument causes the display of the name of the current directory of the specified drive. The CHDIR command does not cause a change to the specified drive, merely a display of the name of the current directory of that drive.

path   This argument causes the current directory to be changed to the one specified by the path. If you try to specify both a new drive and a new path with a single CHDIR command, OS/2 will do nothing.

Default: None

Exit Codes: None

Remarks: The CHDIR command, or its abbreviated form CD, is the best tool for moving from one directory to another on one of your disks. It is also one of two good ways of displaying the current directory. The other good way is to incorporate the current directory path into the system prompt with the batch subcommand PROMPT.

Examples: To change to the root directory:

```
CHDIR \
```

To change to a subdirectory of the root directory named "wordproc":

```
CHDIR \wordproc
```

To change to a *daughter* directory named "letters", immediately below the current directory:

```
CD letters
```

To change to the *parent* directory immediately above the current directory:

```
CD ..
```

Related Commands:
    MKDIR
    PROMPT (batch subcommand)
    RMDIR
    TREE

CHKDSK

Purpose: Checks the directories, files and file allocation table (FAT) on the specified disk drive and produces a status report.

Syntax:

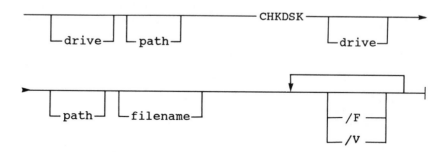

Parameters:

None	Displays a status report showing how disk space is allocated, including space occupied by bad sectors.
/F	Fixes soft errors found on the disk. Soft errors are those in which data is defective, but the disk is not physically damaged.
/V	The *verbose* parameter gives detailed information about errors and displays the paths and names of files as it checks them.

Default:

None	Checks for errors but does not fix them or give a detailed report.

Exit Codes: None

Remarks: You should run the CHKDSK command periodically on your active disks to see if they are beginning to deteriorate. If bad sectors start to appear, use the /F option to recover the lost space.

Since the /F option changes the file allocation table based on information that is specific to a particular disk, do not redirect CHKDSK output when using /F.

When CHKDSK is fixing a disk, it prevents other active processes from accessing the disk until the CHKDSK operation is complete. For this reason, you cannot run the CHKDSK command from the same drive that you are fixing. If you want to fix your hard disk, boot up OS/2 from a floppy in drive A and execute the CHKDSK command from there.

In DOS mode, CHKDSK displays the amount of system memory installed and the amount available as well as the disk status. In OS/2 mode, only disk status is displayed.

As shown in the syntax, you may specify a file or group of files. If you do, in addition to displaying the status report, CHKDSK will also report the number of noncontiguous blocks occupied by the specified file or files. If all specified files are contiguous, CHKDSK will display a statement to that effect.

Examples: Figure 12.1 shows the OS/2 mode status report.

```
  OS/2       Ctrl+Esc = Program Selector                 Type HELP = help
[C:\]chkdsk
Volume OS2 created --  1-3-1988  12:16pm

Errors found.  F parameter not specified.
Corrections will not be written to disk.


18 lost clusters found in 2 chains.
Convert lost chains to files (Y/N)?  n
SYS1359: 36864 bytes disk space would be freed.

 21170176 bytes total disk space.
   260096 bytes in 3 hidden files.
    94208 bytes in 41 directories.
 19093504 bytes in 773 user files.
  1685504 bytes available on disk.

  [C:\]
```

Figure 12.1
OS/2 Mode CHKDSK
Status Report

Figure 12.2 shows the DOS mode status report, incorporating the system memory report.

```
   DOS        Ctrl+Esc = Program Selector                    Type HELP = help
C:\>chkdsk
Volume OS2 created --  1-3-1988   12:16pm

Errors found.  F parameter not specified.
Corrections will not be written to disk.


13 lost clusters found in 1 chains.
Convert lost chains to files (Y/N)?  n
SYS1359: 26624 bytes disk space would be freed.

 21170176 bytes total disk space.
   260096 bytes in 3 hidden files.
    94208 bytes in 41 directories.
 19093504 bytes in 772 user files.
  1695744 bytes available on disk.

[DOS mode storage report]
   654304 bytes total storage
   525216 bytes free

 C:\>
```

Figure 12.2
DOS Mode CHKDSK
Status Report

Related Command:
RECOVER

CLS

Purpose: Clears the display screen.

Syntax:

```
CLS ────────────────────────────────────────────────┤
```

Parameters: None

Default: None

Exit Codes: None

Remarks: Clears the display screen of all except the OS/2 prompt and the cursor.

Example: To clear the screen, type CLS.

Related Commands: None

[O] CMD

Purpose: Starts another command processor in OS/2 mode.

Syntax:

Parameters:

None   Starts a new command processor, which inherits the
              environment of the previous command processor.

/K string   Starts a new command processor, which executes the
              command represented by "string." After execution is
              complete, the new command processor remains active.

/C string   Starts a new command processor, which executes the
              command represented by "string." After execution is
              complete, the new process is terminated and control
              returns to the previous command processor.

Defaults: None

Exit Codes: None

Remarks: When you start a new (secondary) command processor
with the CMD command, it inherits the environment of the previous
(primary) command processor. You can change the environment
variables of the new command processor without affecting the
environment of the previous command processor.

   If the command embedded in the string incorporates command
operators (such as the redirection or piping symbols), then the string
must be enclosed in double quotes. If the string contains no operators,
then the delimiters can be either blank spaces or double quotes.

   If you have not specified the /C parameter for automatic return
to the previous command processor, you can still return to it by
entering the EXIT command. When you invoke the EXIT command
from within a secondary command processor, the secondary process
is terminated and you are returned to the primary command processor.

Examples: You can create a new command processor and have it
display its system prompt by issuing the CMD command with no
parameters:

CMD

You can create a new command processor, have it perform a single command and then disappear by specifying the /C parameter with the command, as in this example:

```
CMD /C CHKDSK A:
```

Related Commands:

COMMAND
EXIT
PROTSHELL (Configuration Command)
START

[D] COMMAND

Purpose: Starts a secondary DOS mode command processor.

Syntax:

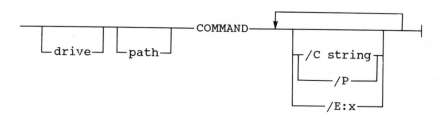

Parameters:

/P   Makes the secondary command processor permanent. To remove it you must reset the system.

/C string   Starts a new command processor, which executes the command represented by "string." After execution is complete, the new process is terminated and control returns to the previous command processor.

/E:x   Specifies the environment size, a number between 160 and 32,768. Any number specified is rounded up to the next highest multiple of sixteen.

Default: The default environment size is 160.

Exit Codes: None

Remarks: The file "command.com" is the DOS mode command processor. Its location in the directory tree is maintained in the environment variable COMSPEC. The value of COMSPEC can be changed with the SET command.

When COMMAND is issued, a new command processor which inherits the environment of the previous command processor is started. You can change the environment of this secondary command processor with the SET command, but when you return to the previous command processor, it still retains its original environment. In other words, changing the environment of the secondary command processor does not affect the environment of the original command processor.

Example: To start a new command processor with an environment size of 8,192, enter the following command:

```
COMMAND /E:8192
```

You are now free to enter any DOS mode commands that you wish (including SET commands that alter the environment of the new command processor). When you are finished with this processor and want to return to your original command processor (with its original environment), merely enter the EXIT command.

Related Commands:

CMD is the OS/2 mode analog of COMMAND.

EXIT releases you from the control of a secondary command processor.

COMP

Purpose: Compares the contents of two files or two groups of files.

Syntax:

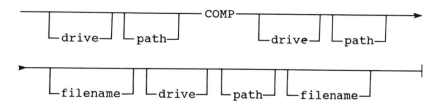

Parameters: None

Default: If no filename is specified, COMP assumes "*.*".

Exit Codes: None

Remarks: With this command, you can compare two files or two groups of files. The comparison is considered successful if the two files are identical on a byte-by-byte basis. You can use global filename characters (wildcards) to specify groups of files. Files may be located on different drives or on the same drive. They may be in different directories or in the same directory. The files may have different filenames or the same filename. Of course, if they have the same filename, they must be in different directories so they can be distinguished from one another. The command,

```
COMP C:\wordproc\*.txt B:*.bak
```

compares every text file in the "wordproc" directory of drive C to a file by the same name in drive B, but with an extension of ".bak" instead of ".txt". The paths and names of the files being compared are displayed on the screen as the comparison proceeds.

If a mismatch is found while two files are being compared, the location of the mismatched byte in the file is displayed, along with the hexadecimal value of that byte in each file. After ten mismatches have been detected and displayed, the comparison is terminated.

COMP is valuable if you have two versions of the same program, but you do not remember exactly what the differences are. COMP will locate and display the first ten bytes that do not match. Often this alone will tell you all you need to know.

If you key in the COMP command without any arguments, OS/2 will prompt you for drive, path, and filename information.

Examples: To compare a file on your hard disk against a file of the same name on a backup floppy, you would use a command like the following:

```
COMP C:\spread\sale4q87.wks A:sale4q87.wks
```

To compare all the worksheet files in the spreadsheet directory of the hard disk with backup files on floppy, you would use this command:

```
COMP C:\spread\*.wks A:
```

Since we do not specify the path and filenames for the second argument, OS/2 assumes that they are the same as the path and filenames in the first argument.

As a third example, we can compare all files in one directory on the hard disk with their corresponding files in another directory on the same hard disk. You may decide to maintain a *shadow* directory that contains up-to-date copies of your working files. This is a form of backup that is quick and easy to perform, but it is not as secure as backing up to removable media. The comparison command in this case would be

```
COMP C:\working C:\shadow
```

Since no individual filenames are specified, all files are compared.

Related Command:
DISKCOMP

COPY

Purpose: Copies one or more files from one location to another. This command can also be used to concatenate (combine) files, or to append one or more files to another.

Syntax: For copying files:

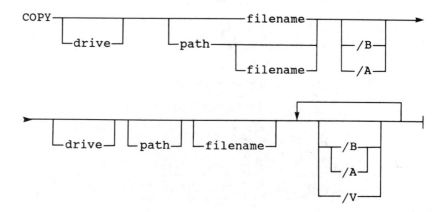

For combining files:

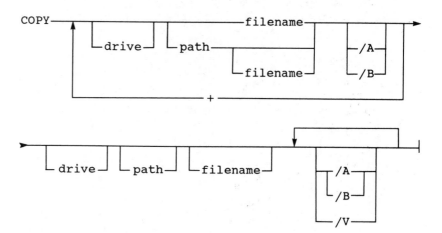

Source File Parameters:

/A   Treats the source file as an ASCII (text) file. The data in the file is copied up to but not including the first end-of-file mark.

/B   Treats the source file as a binary file. All the data in the file is copied, including any end-of-file marks.

Destination File Parameters:

/A   Causes an end-of-file character to be added as the last character of the target file.

/B   Causes no end-of-file character to be added to the target file.

/V   Verifies that all sectors have been properly copied. If the copy operation does not verify, an error message will be displayed.

Defaults:

/B   is the default when files are being copied.

/A   is the default when files are being combined.

Exit Codes: None

Remarks: The COPY command is one of the most versatile of all OS/2 commands. It can be used to copy information from one file or device to another. It can also be used to combine multiple files into one. The exact operation performed will vary depending on how the source and target operands are specified.

If parts of the target operand are not specified, OS/2 makes assumptions about what is desired. Below is a list of the possibilities:

1. The drive, path, and filename of the target file are all specified. In this case, the source file is copied to the specified drive, path, and filename.

2. Only the drive and path of the target file are specified. Here the source filename is retained on the new file that has been copied to the specified drive and path.

3. Only the drive and filename of the target file are specified. The source file is copied to the specified filename in the current directory of the specified drive.

4. Only the drive is specified for the target file. The source file is copied with its original filename to the current directory of the specified drive.

5. Only a path is specified for the target file. The source file is copied with its original filename to the specified directory of the default drive.

6. Only a filename is specified for the target file. The source file is copied to the specified filename in the current directory of the default drive.

7. No second operand is specified. In this case, the source file is copied with its original filename to the current directory of the default drive. If the source drive is also the default drive,

the COPY operation will halt with an error message since
OS/2 will not allow you to copy a file onto itself.

You can combine (concatenate) multiple source files into a single
target file by specifying all the source files, separated by plus (+)
signs. Files are normally combined in ASCII mode (/A is the default).
This causes the end-of-file mark of each source file to *not* be copied to
the destination file. The target file will be terminated by the physical
end-of-file instead. Binary files may be combined with ASCII files by
using both /B and /A parameters.

The /A and /B parameters take effect on the file that immediately precedes them on the command line. Once specified, a parameter
remains in effect for subsequent filenames in that operand until it is
superceded by the specification of another parameter.

Normally, when you copy a file to a file with a new filename, the
date and time stored with the new file are the current date and time
for the COPY operation. On the other hand, if you copy a file without
changing its name, the date and time recorded in the directory for the
new file remain the same as the date and time of the original file. You
can override this default and update the date and time to the time of
the COPY operation even though the filename is unchanged. This is
accomplished by using the plus (+) symbol followed by two commas
after the source file specification. For example, to copy a file named
"document.txt" in the current directory of the default drive to a file
with the same name on the floppy in drive A, updating the new file's
date and time to the current values, use the following command:

```
COPY document.txt + ,, A:
```
To do the same thing to a binary file named "progfile.asm" you must
also specify the /B parameter to assure proper handling of the end-
of-file character:

```
COPY progfile.asm /B + ,, A:
```

Examples: We discussed the COPY command early in this book when
we described how to create a batch file directly from the console with
the COPY command. We created the following simple batch file:

```
COPY con prog1.cmd/A
:START
ECHO Program 1 is running.
GOTO START
^Z
```

The /A parameter was used to place an end-of-file character at the
end of the file. If we had not included the /A parameter, the default
value of /B for a copy operation would have been used, and the file

"prog1.cmd" would not have been properly terminated. It would probably execute properly in either case, but there might be problems with the unterminated file. If you loaded it into a text editor like WordStar, you would see a string of "garbage characters" following the last statement in the file. This unwanted data would not be present if the file were properly terminated after its last statement.

To combine files, use the plus sign in the following manner:

`COPY chap1.txt + chap2.txt + chap3.txt book.txt`

The three chapter files are concatenated into one book file. To append more chapters to the book file, specify the new chapters along with the already existing book file:

`COPY book.txt + chap4.txt + chap5.txt + chapt6.txt`

Since you do not specify the name of the destination file, OS/2 assumes it is the same as the first file named, "book.txt". It adds Chapters 4 through 6 to the three chapters that already are included in the book file.

Related Commands:
DISKCOPY
RENAME
VERIFY
XCOPY

[O] CREATEDD

Purpose: Creates a dump diskette to be used in troubleshooting system problems.

Syntax:

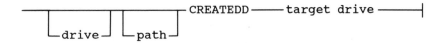

Parameters:

target drive   The diskette drive containing the diskette to be formatted as a dump diskette.

Default: None

Exit Codes: None

Remarks: This command prepares a diskette to be used as a diagnostic dump diskette. It should be used only in consultation with a skilled technician. By inserting this diskette in a floppy drive and depressing a sequence of keys on the keyboard, you can cause the entire contents of system memory to be "dumped" to a sequence of diskettes for analysis. CREATEDD uses the FORMAT command, which must be present in the current directory or along the currently active path. Since CREATEDD uses FORMAT in a special way to create a single dump disk, when FORMAT prompts you, "Format another?" respond with "N". Another unusual effect of the CREATEDD command is that it makes the dump disk appear to be full. This prevents you from inadvertently copying files over top of a system dump. Once a dump diskette has been created, the only way to write on it is to actually perform a dump. If you ever want to use that diskette in the normal way again, you will have to reformat it.

The diskette created by CREATEDD is used only to start the dump. You must also have a supply of blank or reusable diskettes available to accommodate all the data contained in your system memory. If these additional diskettes are unformatted, they will be formatted "on the fly" just before the contents of memory is copied to them.

If possible, bring all other processes to a stop before performing a dump. While the dump is in progress, all other system activity is halted. This suspension of execution may affect some types of tasks if it occurs in the middle of a critical function.

To start a dump with a dump diskette that was configured for use in drive A, insert the dump disk into drive A. Then, while depressing the Ctrl and Alt keys, press the Num Lock key twice. A dump can be started from either DOS or OS/2 mode, although the dump disk can only be created in OS/2 mode.

Once you have started the dump, all of system memory is copied, starting from address zero. No time or space is wasted copying storage that has not been installed, but all existing memory is dumped. The minimum dump size is one megabyte.

You may end the dump before all memory has been copied by reinserting the dump diskette when you are prompted to insert another diskette. The system will recognize the diskette and abort the dump operation.

Examples: To create a dump diskette to be used in drive A, insert a blank floppy into drive A and enter

```
CREATEDD A:
```

Related Commands:

TRACE statement in "config.sys"
TRACEBUF statement in "config.sys"
TRACE
TRACEFMT

DATE

Purpose: Displays or changes the system date.

Syntax:

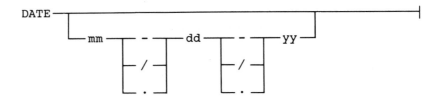

Parameters:

mm   Month must be a number between 1 and 12.

dd   Day must be a number between 1 and 31.

yy   Year must be a number between 80 and 79, or between 1980 and 2079.

Separators may be either dashes, slashes, or periods.

Defaults: None

Exit Codes: None

Remarks: The format of the date may vary in countries other than the United States. Refer to the COUNTRY command for differences.

If you enter the DATE command without parameters, OS/2 displays the date and gives you the opportunity to enter a new date. If you enter the DATE command with a new date parameter, OS/2 changes the system date to the new value but does not display it.

Examples: To display the current date, enter

    `DATE`

OS/2 will display

    `The current date is Sunday 12-27-1987`
    `Enter the new date: (mm-dd-yy):_`

If you press the Enter key at this point, the date will not be changed.

To change the date without displaying it first, enter a new date parameter:

    `DATE 2-29-88`

The computer's internal clock will be changed to reflect a new system date of February 29, 1988.

Related Commands:

    COUNTRY statement in "config.sys"
    TIME

DEL

Purpose: Deletes files from disks. DEL is another name for the ERASE command. See ERASE for a complete description.

[O] DETACH

Purpose: Starts a noninteractive program running in the background.

Syntax:

DETACH ——————————— command ———————————————————|

Parameters:

command   Any program or external OS/2 command that does not require input from the keyboard or mouse, and that does not output to the display screen.

Default: None

Exit Codes: None

Remarks: When you issue the DETACH command, OS/2 starts an independent process for the program that has been detached, then returns to the command prompt. You can start another process in the foreground while the detached process operates in the background. The detached process must not depend on any input from the keyboard or the mouse. It must not send any output to the screen. Finally, it must be able to come to a natural termination without operator intervention.

You can run background processes that normally access the keyboard or the screen by redirecting input or output. If you redirect input to a file that contains a sequence of keystrokes or redirect output to a file that holds screen images, the process can be run in the background. You must be careful, however, not to detach a program that uses the keyboard or screen. To do so might ruin files being used by another process.

Examples: You may wish to sort a large directory alphabetically by filename and save the sorted directory in a file. This can be done in the background with the following command:

```
DETACH DIR | SORT > director.srt
```

The detached DIR command is piped to the SORT filter, then redirected to a file named "director.srt". Since the output goes to a disk file rather than the screen, background execution is permissible.

Related Command:

RUN statement in "config.sys".

DIR

Purpose: Lists the files in a directory and displays the number of files listed. Subdirectories are listed also since they are a special type of file.

Syntax: The syntax of the DOS mode DIR command is somewhat different from the syntax of the OS/2 mode DIR command.

[D] (DOS Mode)

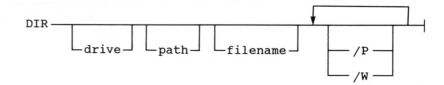

[O] (OS/2 Mode)

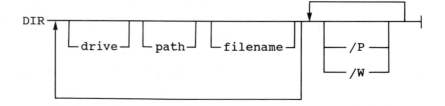

Parameters:

None   The entire directory is displayed, one line after another, where each line is a directory entry consisting of the filename, filesize in bytes, and the date and time of the last file modification.

/P   Causes the directory listing to pause after a screenful has been displayed. It allows the user to examine the display thoroughly before proceeding to show the next screenful.

/W   Causes a wide directory to be displayed in which up to five columns of filenames are shown instead of a single column of filenames with associated file sizes and the date and time of the last file modification.

Default: If no argument is specified, DIR lists all files in the current directory of the default drive.

Exit Codes: None

Remarks: The DIR command is used to show what files are on a disk. It also gives information about the sizes of the files and about when they were created or last modified.

The syntax of the DOS mode version differs from the syntax of the OS/2 mode version. Only one argument specifying one or more files in a single subdirectory may be used with the DOS mode version. Multiple arguments may be used with the OS/2 version, specifying one or more files in multiple, unrelated directories, and even on different disk drives.

Global filename characters, or wildcards (? and *) may be used as part of the file specification. In general, when no filename or extension is specified, it is assumed that all filenames or extensions satisfy the criteria. Thus:

DIR	is equivalent to	DIR *.*
DIR filename	is equivalent to	DIR filename.*
DIR .ext	is equivalent to	DIR *.ext

If the COUNTRY command in the "config.sys" file is set for a country other than the United States, the directory date and time formats may differ from those shown below.

Examples: In OS/2 mode, if you issue the following command,

```
DIR test shell
```

the system will display the volume label of the default drive, the name of the default directory, the information on the "test" and "shell" files, and the amount of free space on the default disk. Here's a possible display:

```
Volume in drive A is OS2_PROGRAM
Directory of A:\
TEST        BAT          13 11-15-87  2:47p
TEST        DAT        2677 11-15-87  6:47p
TEST        CMD         126 11-29-87  9:59p

SHELL       EXE       27732 8-01-87 12:00a
SHELL       LIB       17304 8-01-87 12:00a
        5 File(s)        114688 bytes free
```

In this case we see that the default drive, a floppy, had three files with a filename of "test" and two with a filename of "shell".

If you want to list files that have no extension, rather than those that have any extension, you must explicitly show the period that separates the filename from the extension. Quite often I want to list all the subdirectories in the current directory. Since I follow the convention of always giving files an extension and never giving subdirectories an extension, I can list all subdirectories of the current directory with the following command:

    DIR *.

Only files with no extension will be listed. Because of my naming conventions, they will all be subdirectories.

If a directory has 20 entries or fewer, you will not need to use either the /P or the /W parameter. The entire directory listing will fit on your screen. However, if you have more than 20 entries, you may want to use the /P parameter, the /W parameter, or both. The /W parameter will let you put 100 filenames on the screen at once, but it will not show filesize or creation date information. The /P parameter will show no more than 21 entries at once, but it will not scroll any of them off the top of the display until you press a key on the keyboard.

Related Command:

COUNTRY statement in "config.sys"

DISKCOMP

Purpose: Compares the diskette in the source drive to the diskette in the target drive.

Syntax:

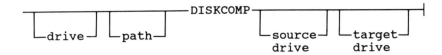

Parameters: None

Default: If you do not specify the source drive, the target drive, or both, the default drive is assumed.

Exit Codes:

0   Compared OK. The disks compared exactly.

1   Did not compare. The disks are not the same.

2   Terminated by user (Ctrl-C).

3   Hard error. A nonrecoverable read or write error occurred— compare unsuccessful.

4   Initialization error. Incorrect command syntax or not enough memory.

Remarks: This command performs a track-by-track comparison of one diskette to another. Even if you have only one floppy disk drive, you can still compare two diskettes by alternately inserting them into and removing them from the disk drive. If DISKCOMP detects a mismatch, it issues an error message indicating the track and disk side (0 or 1) where the mismatch occurred.

Because OS/2 is a multitasking environment, it is possible that one process might attempt to alter the data on one of the diskettes installed on the system while another process is trying to perform a DISKCOMP. To prevent problems, OS/2 locks the diskettes, preventing any program from reading or writing the diskettes while the DISKCOMP is in progress.

If you use the COPY command to copy the contents of one disk to another, there is a good chance that DISKCOMP will not find the two disks to be identical. OS/2 may rearrange the placement of files on the target disk. The DISKCOPY command, however, will copy the files track by track. The file arrangement will be identical, and DISKCOMP should verify that fact.

Although it is possible to have floppy disk drives of different capacities attached to the same computer, you can only use DISK-COMP to compare diskettes that have exactly the same capacity. You may compare a diskette inserted into a 1.2Mb capacity drive with a diskette inserted into a 360K capacity drive, as long as both diskettes are 360K diskettes.

Examples: Compare the diskette inserted into floppy drive A with the diskette inserted into floppy drive B with the following command:

```
DISKCOMP A: B:
```

If you issue the DISKCOMP command without parameters, OS/2 will compare the source disk installed in the default drive against the target disk, also installed in the default drive. OS/2 will prompt you to change disks repeatedly as it reads first one and then the other.

Related Commands:
COMP
DISKCOPY

DISKCOPY

Purpose: Copies the entire contents of a source diskette to a target diskette, on a track-by-track basis. If the target diskette is unformatted, DISKCOPY performs the format during the copy operation.

Syntax:

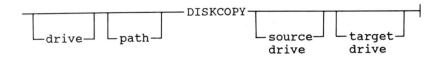

Parameters: None

Default: None

Exit Codes:

0   Copied successfully.

1   Nonfatal read or write error. A nonrecoverable, but nonfatal read or write error occurred.

2   Terminated by user (Ctrl-C).

3   Fatal hard error. Unable to read the source disk or format the target disk.

4   Initialization error. Improper command syntax or insufficient memory.

Remarks: This command copies the entire contents of one diskette onto another, on a track-by-track basis. It is possible to do a one-drive DISKCOPY by alternately placing the source and the target diskettes into the specified drive. The diskettes are compared a block at a time.

Because OS/2 is a multitasking operating system, it is possible that one process might try to alter the contents of a diskette while another process is attempting to perform a DISKCOPY on that diskette. To prevent such problems, OS/2 locks up both the source and the target disk drives so that they cannot be read or written until the DISKCOPY operation is complete.

If DISKCOPY detects an error, it issues a message indicating the drive, side, and track where the error occurred.

Although it is possible to have floppy disk drives of different capacities attached to the same computer, you can only use DISK-COPY to copy diskettes that have exactly the same capacity. You may copy a diskette inserted into a 1.2Mb capacity drive to a diskette inserted into a 360K capacity drive, as long as both diskettes are 360K diskettes.

Examples: To copy the diskette in drive A onto a blank floppy in drive B, issue the command,

```
DISKCOPY A: B:
```

You may use this same syntax even if you have only one diskette drive on your system. OS/2 will alternately apply the designators A and B to your drive, and it will instruct you to swap source and target diskettes when the designator changes.

Related Commands:
COPY
XCOPY
DISKCOMP

[O] DPATH

Purpose: Specifies directories outside the current directory that will be searched for data files.

Syntax: To specify the paths to data files outside the current directory:

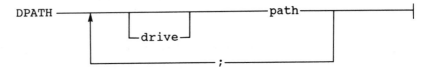

To display the paths to data files that are currently in effect:

DPATH ————————————————————————————————————

To remove all paths to data files that have previously been set:

DPATH ————————————— ; ——————————————————

Parameters: None

Default: No path

Exit Codes: None

Remarks: The DPATH command gives you access to data files outside the current directory in OS/2 mode in the same manner that APPEND gives you access to data files in DOS mode. DPATH is a system environment variable, which means it can be changed by the SET command as well as by the DPATH command.

You can specify as many directories as you want in a DPATH command up to the maximum number of characters that will fit on a command line (128).

Every time you issue a DPATH command, OS/2 replaces whatever data path may have been in effect with the new one that you have specified in the command.

Examples: To display the current data path, issue the DPATH command with no path information:

    DPATH

The current data path will be displayed on the screen.

To cancel whatever data path is currently in effect, issue the DPATH command followed by a semicolon:

```
DPATH ;
```

The system will revert to the default condition of no data path.

When you install OS/2, the installation procedure creates a batch file named "os2init.cmd" that is run every time the system is powered up or reset. It contains a DPATH command that sets the following data path:

```
DPATH C:\;C:os2;C:\os2\install;
```

Thus, regardless of what the current directory is, you will have direct access to data files in the root directory of drive C as well as in the "\os2" and the "\os2\install" subdirectories.

If you want to merely add a new directory to the already existing data path rather than discarding the old path, you can do so using a replaceable parameter. For example, say you want to add the directory "C:\wordproc" to the data path set by the "os2inst.cmd" file. Use the following command:

```
DPATH %DPATH%C:\wordproc;
```

The first DPATH is the command. The second DPATH, surrounded by percent signs, is the environment variable. The percent signs tell OS/2 to use the contents of the environment variable DPATH for this part of the command. Last is the specification of the directory you are adding to the path. This command has the same effect as if you had typed the entire path:

```
DPATH C:\;C:\os2;C:\os2\install;C:\wordproc;
```

Related Commands:
APPEND
PATH
SET

ERASE

Purpose: Deletes specified files from the specified directory.

Syntax:

[D]

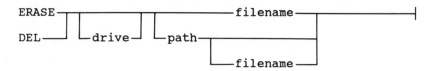

[O]

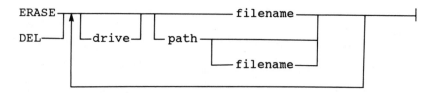

Parameters: None

Default: Delete all the files in the current directory of the default drive.

Exit Codes: None

Remarks: The ERASE command works exactly the same regardless of whether you use the ERASE or the DEL syntax. In DOS mode, you can use the ERASE command to delete one or more files in a single directory on a single drive. In OS/2 mode, one ERASE command can delete files in multiple directories on multiple drives.

You may use wildcard characters to specify multiple files for deletion. To delete all the files in the current directory, type

    DEL *.*

or just

    DEL

Since this is a fairly drastic thing to do, OS/2 gives you a chance to reconsider by responding:

    Are you sure (Y/N)?

If you type "Y", OS/2 proceeds with the deletion. If you type "N", OS/2 returns you to the system prompt. If you are like me, sometimes your fingers type faster than your brain thinks. This little safety feature of OS/2 may save you from mistakenly erasing files you want to keep.

Examples: To erase a file named "smith.let" from the current directory, type

```
DEL smith.let
```

To erase all backup files from the directory "\wordproc", type

```
DEL \wordproc\*.bak
```

To erase all text files from the "\letters" subdirectory on your hard disk and from the root directory of the diskette installed in your A drive, type

```
ERASE C:\letters\*.txt A:\*.txt
```

Related Commands: None

EXIT

Purpose: Ends the current command processor and returns you to the previous command processor.

Syntax:

```
EXIT ─────────────────────────────────────────────────────────┤
```

Parameters: None

Default: None

Exit Codes: None

Remarks: Use this command to terminate a process after the application in it has run to completion. If your current process is a "child" of an already existing process, typing EXIT will return you to the "parent" process. You can create an OS/2 mode child process by entering CMD at the system prompt. A new command processor will be created that inherits the environment of the parent process.

If the current OS/2 mode process was invoked from the Session Manager screen, rather than being created from within a running process, the EXIT command will return you to the Session Manager screen. If you issue the EXIT command from within the top level DOS mode command processor, nothing happens. You must press Ctrl-Esc to return to the Session Manager Screen.

Examples: To return from a lower level (child) command processor to a higher level (parent) command processor, issue the command,

    EXIT

Related Commands:
    COMMAND
    CMD

[O] FDISK

Purpose: Creates, changes, and deletes hard disk partitions. It also displays the current partitioning of the hard disks connected to the system.

Syntax:

Parameters: None

Default: If more than one hard disk drive is connected to the system, FDISK selects the first.

Exit Codes: None

Remarks: With FDISK, you can create a primary partition. The primary partition contains system files and is the partition that the system boots from at power-up or after the system is reset. You can also create an extended partition which may contain one or more logical drives. Each logical drive seems to be a separate disk drive, even though in fact it may merely be a different area on your system hard disk.

You may have another operating system (e.g. Unix) in a separate partition of your hard disk in addition to having OS/2 in the primary partition. If so, you can use FDISK to cause the system to boot into Unix instead of OS/2. This is done with the "change active partition" function of FDISK.

Just as FDISK gives you the power to create partitions and logical drives, it also allows you to delete them. The display function lets you see the current organization of partitions and logical drives, allowing you to decide whether you want to change the current setup in any way.

No programs other than FDISK should be running whenever you are creating or deleting partitions or logical drives. Once a disk has been repartitioned with FDISK, any data that had previously been on the disk will be inaccessible. Normally, after a disk has been partitioned with FDISK, it must be formatted with FORMAT before it becomes usable.

In OS/2 Version 1.0, the primary partition may be no larger than 32Mb. No logical drive in the extended partition may be larger than 32Mb. This restriction is caused by a limitation in the file allocation table (FAT) structure of OS/2. If you have a hard disk that is larger than 32Mb, you must divide it up into logical drives of 32Mb or less. Version 1.1 of OS/2 allows disk partitions to be up to 314Mb in size.

Examples: To examine or change disk partitions on a system that already has an operational OS/2 system on it, type

        F D I S K

at the OS/2 command prompt.

Related Command:
        FORMAT

FIND

Purpose: FIND is a filter that searches for a specific text string in a file or a group of files.

Syntax:

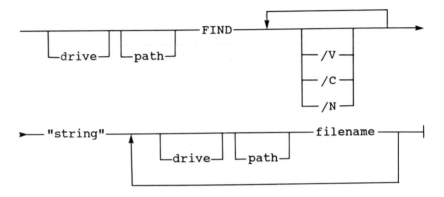

Parameters:

None   Displays all lines containing the specified string.

/V   Displays all lines not containing the specified string.

/C   Displays only the number of lines (count) that contain a match. If /V is also specified, then /C displays the number of lines that do not contain a match.

/N   Displays the relative line number in front of every line that contains a match. If /C is also specified, the /N parameter is ignored.

string   Specifies the search string. The string must be enclosed in double quotes.

Default: If no search string is specified in the command line, FIND expects the string to be entered from the keyboard. If neither /V, /C, nor /N is specified, FIND displays every line in the specified file or files that contains the search string.

Exit Codes: None

Remarks: FIND searches a specified group of files for a specified text string. Every time it finds the string, it displays the line that contains it on the screen.

The FIND filter is case sensitive. A word in upper case will not match the same word in lower case or in a combination of upper and lower case.

Wildcards (? and *) may not be used in the specification of the files to be searched. Each filename must be explicitly specified.

FIND may get its input directly from a file, or it may get it from a pipe.

Examples: Let's say you have started writing a book in which you have used the words "protected mode." After writing two chapters, you decide that it would be better to use the words "OS/2 mode" instead. To see how many times the obsolete phrase occurred in the chapters you have already written, type

```
FIND /C "protected mode"
    c:\ws\chap1.txt c:\ws\chap2.txt
```

Then type

```
FIND /C "Protected Mode"
    c:\ws\chap1.txt c:\ws\chap2.txt
```

Since the comparison done by the FIND command is case sensitive, you must specify every variation of capitalization that might appear in the document. You specified the /C parameter in the above commands, so FIND will return only the count (the number of lines in which the search string occurred).

Related Command:
    COMP

FORMAT

Purpose: Prepares a hard disk or diskette to accept OS/2 system files and data files.

Syntax:

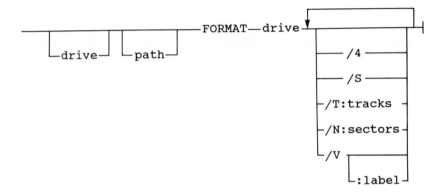

Parameters:

/4
Formats a 360K diskette in a 1.2Mb drive. Disks formatted in this way cannot be reliably read in a 360K drive.

/S
Copies the operating system files listed in the "formats.tbl" file on the default drive to the newly formatted disk.

/T:tracks
Specifies the number of tracks to be formatted. 360K diskettes have 40 tracks, 720K, 1.2Mb, and 1.44Mb diskettes all have 80 tracks.

/N:sectors
Specifies the number of sectors per track. 360K and 720K diskettes have 9 sectors per track. 1.2Mb diskettes have 15 sectors per track, and 1.44Mb diskettes have 18 sectors per track.

/V
Specifies the volume label, which can be up to 11 characters long. If you do not specify a volume label, you will be prompted for one after the format operation is complete.

Default: You must specify the drive to be formatted, but all other parameters are optional. If you are formatting a diskette, the default assumption is that the diskette has the same capacity as the drive it is installed in, and you want to format it to its maximum possible size.

System files will not be transferred to the newly formatted diskette. If you are formatting a hard disk, the entire logical drive specified will be formatted, and system files will not be transferred.

Exit Codes:

0   Successful completion.

3   Terminated by user (Ctrl-C).

4   Fatal error.

5   N response to prompt, "Proceed with format (Y/N)?".

Remarks: The FORMAT command initializes the directory and the file allocation tables (FATs) on a disk. Before the FORMAT command can operate, an OS/2 partition or an IBM Personal Computer DOS partition must exist on the disk. See the FDISK command for creating disk partitions.

When you transfer system files using the /S parameter, OS/2 expects all system files to be present in the root directory of the default disk. If all system files are not present, you must copy them to the new disk after the format is complete. The names of these system files are contained in the file "formats.tbl".

As a safety feature, OS/2 prompts you for the volume label of the hard disk to be formatted. If you do not enter the correct volume label, OS/2 will not format the drive. If you do enter the correct volume label, OS/2 will display

```
WARNING, ALL DATA ON NON-REMOVABLE DISK
DRIVE X: WILL BE LOST!
Proceed with Format (Y/N)?
```

Enter a "Y" at this point to start the format. If you now realize that there is data on the drive that you want to keep, enter "N" to abort the format operation.

Normally, the FORMAT command will attempt to format a diskette up to the maximum capacity of the drive into which it is inserted. You can use the /T and /N parameters to format lower capacity diskettes in higher capacity drives. Use Table 12.1 to determine parameters when formatting a 360K diskette in a 1.2Mb drive or a 720K diskette in a 1.44Mb drive. You may format a 360K diskette in a 1.2Mb drive by specifying the proper /T and /N parameters, but it is easier and just as effective to specify the /4 parameter.

To assure that you do not exceed the maximum number of root directory entries shown in the table, create subdirectories for your data files.

Table 12.1
Diskette FORMAT
Parameters

Diskette Type	/N: Number of Sectors per Track	/T: Track Count	# of Root Directory Entries
5.25-inch 360K	9	40	112
5.25-inch 1.2Mb	15	80	224
3.5-inch 720K	9	80	112
3.5-inch 1.44Mb	18	80	224

Restrictions: FORMAT ignores any drive reassignments made with the ASSIGN, JOIN, and SUBST commands. It will also refuse to format a drive over a network. Do not use the FORMAT command if drive reassignments are in effect or if the drive is accessed via a network.

Examples: To format a diskette where the capacity of the diskette is the same as the capacity of the A drive, enter

```
FORMAT A:
```
To format a 720K diskette in a 1.44Mb A drive, enter
```
FORMAT A: /N:9
```
To format a 360K diskette in a 1.2Mb A drive, enter
```
FORMAT A: /4
```
To format your primary hard disk and transfer system files to it, enter
```
FORMAT C: /S
```

Related Commands:
LABEL
SYS
VOL

[D] GRAFTABL

Purpose: Allows an extended character set (ASCII characters 128 to 255) to be displayed on the graphics display operating in graphics mode.

Syntax:

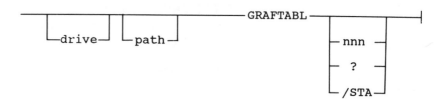

Parameters:

nnn   The three-digit number of the code page to be used to supply the extended character set, where:

         437 is the U.S. code page
         860 is the Portuguese code page
         863 is the Canadian-French code page
         865 is the Nordic code page

?   Displays the number of the current code page and the available options for the GRAFTABL command.

/STA   Displays the number of the current graphic code page, if one has been invoked.

Default: The U.S. code page (number 437) is the default code page.

Exit Codes:

0   Command successful.

1   Table already loaded.

2   File error occurred.

Remarks: GRAFTABL only has an effect on DOS mode operation when using either the Color Graphics Adapter, the Enhanced Graphics Adapter, or the Video Graphics Array, in modes 4, 5, and 6 (the graphics modes).

When you load graphics characters with GRAFTABL, the size of OS/2 is increased, reducing the amount of memory available for applications. Once a graphics table has been loaded, it cannot be changed or removed without rebooting the system. If you will be using extended graphics characters regularly, you should put a

GRAFTABL command in your "autoexec.bat" or "os2init.cmd" start-up batch files. The graphics table will be loaded automatically at the start of your work day.

Examples: To load the default graphics table (U.S. version) enter
GRAFTABL
To see which graphics table is loaded enter
GRAFTABL /STA
To load the Nordic graphics table enter
GRAFTABL 865

Related Command:
CHCP

HELP

Purpose: Displays a line of help text, a screenful of help text, or information about specific warning or error messages.

Syntax:

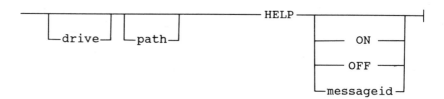

Parameters:

None	Displays the help screen.
ON	Turns on the display of the help line.
OFF	Turns off the display of the help line.
messageid	Identifies the message about which information is being requested.

Default: If no parameters are specified, the help screen is displayed. It gives information about how to switch between sessions and how to get help information.

Exit Codes: None

Remarks: Whenever OS/2 is unable to successfully execute a command, it displays a message on the screen. Often the message is descriptive enough for you to determine what went wrong. If not, you can get additional explanation of the message by issuing a HELP command, including the message number as a parameter.

Examples: In the process of entering a command, you have mistyped a filename. OS/2 returns the following error message:

```
SYS0002: The system cannot find the
    file specified.
```

To explain the message further, type

```
HELP 2
```

You could also have typed HELP SYS0002, or HELP SYS2, or HELP SYS02, etc. The result would have been the same in any of these cases. OS/2 would display the following message:

```
SYS0002: The system cannot find the
    file specified.
```

```
EXPLANATION: The file named in the
command does not exist in the
current directory or search path
specified. Or, the filename was
entered incorrectly.
ACTION: Retry the command using the
correct filename.
```

If the original message contained variable data such as a filename, that data is represented by three asterisks (***) when the message is redisplayed above the explanation.

Related Command:
HELPMSG

HELPMSG

Purpose: Displays a screenful of help text or information about specific warning or error messages.

Syntax:

Parameters:

None	Displays the help screen.
messageid	Identifies the message about which information is being requested.

Default: If no parameters are specified, the help screen is displayed. It gives information about how to switch between sessions and how to get help information.

Exit Codes: None

Remarks: The HELPMSG command is a subset of the HELP command. It acts just like the HELP command, except it does not accept the ON or the OFF parameter. Thus it cannot be used to determine whether or not to display the help line.

Related Command:
    HELP

[D] JOIN

Purpose: Logically connects a disk drive to a subdirectory on another disk drive.

Syntax:

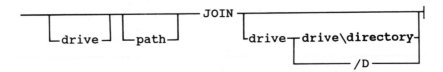

Parameters:

None	Displays which drives are currently joined.
drive drive \ directory	The drive specified first is identified as "\ directory" on the drive specified second.
drive /D	Turns off any joins currently in effect.

Default: None

Exit Codes: None

Remarks: This command allows you to treat files on one drive (called the *guest drive*) as if they were contained in a subdirectory of a second drive (called the *host drive*). You can use JOIN to treat a floppy disk or a RAM disk as if it were a subdirectory on your hard disk.

There are several restrictions on the use of JOIN. The guest drive can only be joined to a subdirectory of the root directory of the host drive. In addition, that directory must be empty, or the JOIN command will not work. If the directory specified in the JOIN command does not exist, JOIN creates it.

Since JOIN alters the logical structure of your system, it creates some incompatibilities. Several OS/2 commands do not work when dealing with a joined disk drive. Other commands work, but must be handled with special care. The following commands do not work on a drive that has been joined:

    CHKDSK
    DISKCOPY
    FDISK
    FORMAT
    LABEL
    RECOVER
    SYS

In addition, the BACKUP, RESTORE, DISKCOMP, and DISKCOPY commands will not work as you would expect. You should either avoid them or disable the JOIN before using them. Since the SUBST and ASSIGN commands affect the identification of disk drives in much the same way that the JOIN command does, they should not be used with it either.

Examples: To join a floppy disk which contains data files and is installed in drive A to a subdirectory on your hard disk, type

```
JOIN A: C:\datafile
```

After you are finished using the joined drives, disable the JOIN with

```
JOIN A: /D
```

Related Commands:
SUBST
ASSIGN

[O] KEYB xx

Purpose: Selects an alternate keyboard layout to replace the default U.S. keyboard layout.

Syntax:

Parameters:

layout   Specifies the desired keyboard layout with a two character code. The table below shows the available choices:

xx	Keyboard Layout
BE	Belgium
CF	Canada (French)
DK	Denmark
SU	Finland
FR	France
GR	Germany
IT	Italy
LA	Latin America
NL	Netherlands
NO	Norway
PO	Portugal
SP	Spain
SV	Sweden
SF	Switzerland (French)
SG	Switzerland (German)
UK	United Kingdom
US	United States

Default: The U.S. keyboard layout is the default.

Exit Codes: None

Remarks: People in different countries are accustomed to different keyboard layouts. The KEYB command allows OS/2 to reconfigure the keyboard to the layout appropriate for a given country. Although the letters engraved on the keycaps do not change, these keys now produce the characters appropriate for the country of use, rather than the default U.S. characters.

In order for the KEYB command to work properly, you must have included CODEPAGE, COUNTRY, and DEVINFO statements in your "config.sys" file that support the country whose keyboard you want to use. If the correct DEVINFO statement has not been issued, you will receive a warning message when you execute the KEYB command.

Many languages make use of accented characters. For those languages where accents are used, you can create an accented character with two keystrokes. First type the accent, then type the letter. The two characters will be superimposed. If you want to type the accent by itself, you will have to press the space bar after typing the accent mark, to get the cursor to advance to the next character position.

Although the KEYB command must be issued in OS/2 mode, its effects carry over into DOS mode as well.

Examples: To use the Canadian French keyboard layout, be sure the following statements are in your "config.sys" file:

```
CODEPAGE=863,850
COUNTRY=002
DEVINFO=KBD,CF,C:\keyboard.dcp
```

Related Commands:
    CODEPAGE statement in "config.sys"
    COUNTRY statement in "config.sys"
    DEVINFO statement in "config.sys"
    DATE
    TIME

LABEL

Purpose: Creates or changes the volume label on a disk.

Syntax:

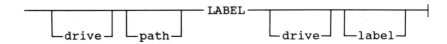

Parameters:

label   The volume label that identifies the disk. It may be up to
            11 characters in length. Any character that is allowed for
            a filename is also allowed for a volume label.

Default: If you do not specify a volume label for a disk, the disk will
have no label.

Exit Codes: None

Remarks: You can specify a volume label for a disk or diskette as a
parameter of the LABEL command. If you issue the LABEL command
without a parameter, OS/2 will prompt you for a volume label for the
default drive. You may respond by entering a new volume label or by
pressing the Enter key. If you press the Enter key, the volume label
will not be updated.

Do not use the LABEL command when the ASSIGN, JOIN, and
SUBST commands are in effect since there is some ambiguity at those
times as to which disk is which.

Examples: You have a diskette named "newmemos" that you want to
relabel to "oldmemos". If you are sure that the diskette installed in
drive A is the proper one, you can perform the relabel in a single
operation with this command:

```
LABEL A:oldmemos
```
However, if you want to confirm that the diskette you have chosen is
indeed the "newmemos" diskette, issue the command without the
label parameter:

```
LABEL A:
```
OS/2 will respond with the message:

```
The volume label in drive A is
  NEWMEMOS.
Enter a volume label of up to
  11 characters or press Enter for
  no volume label update.
```

Then enter:
    oldmemos

Related Commands:
    FORMAT
    VOL

MKDIR

Purpose: Makes a new subdirectory.

Syntax:

[D]

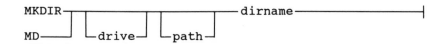

[O]

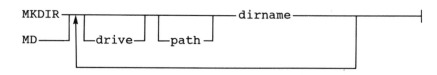

Parameters:

dirname   The name of the new subdirectory you are making. It must not be the same as the filename of any file in the same directory.

Defaults: If no drive is specified, the default drive is assumed.

If no path is specified, OS/2 assumes that the new directory will be a subdirectory of the current directory.

Exit Codes: None

Remarks: Both the MKDIR and the MD forms of the command perform identically. In OS/2 mode, multiple directories can be made with a single command.

Examples: In DOS mode, you can create a family of directories for an operator named Bill, as follows:

```
MKDIR C:\bill
MKDIR C:\bill\memos
MKDIR C:\bill\letters
MKDIR C:\bill\database
```

In OS/2 mode with drive C as the default drive, you can create the same directories with a single command:

```
MD \bill \bill\memos \bill\letters \bill\database
```

Related Commands:
  CHDIR
  DIR
  RMDIR
  TREE

MODE

The MODE command is used in several different ways, and its syntax varies depending on how it is used. We will give a command syntax diagram for each of the major uses.

Purpose: Sets operation parameters for the asynchronous ports, the display, the printer ports, and the diskettes.

Syntax: For use with asynchronous communications ports:
[O] To set OS/2 asynchronous communications modes:

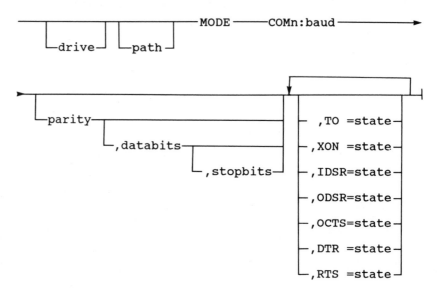

NOTE: This form of the MODE command will only work if the device driver "com0x.sys" is installed, where "x" is the number of the COM port.

[D] To set DOS asynchronous communications modes:

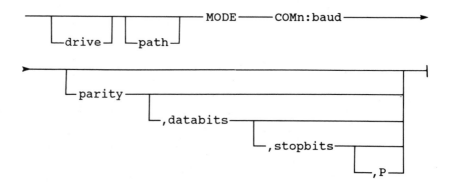

NOTE: The positions of the parity, databits, stopbits, and P parameters are significant. If you accept the default value of one or more of these parameters, you still must mark its place with a comma. Thus, to accept the default values for the parity, databits, and stopbits parameter, but to specify the P parameter, syntax would be similar to the following:

`MODE COM2:9600,,,P`

You may set asynchronous communications modes from either OS/2 mode or DOS mode. However, since some serial devices require parameters that are available only in OS/2 mode, it is a good practice to do all asynchronous communications settings from OS/2 mode.

[O] To query asynchronous communications port status in OS/2 mode:

NOTE: With this form of the MODE command, you can determine what the current settings are of the communications port parameters. The output of a query of the form

`MODE COM1`

can be redirected, modified, or used as input to another MODE command.

Parameters: For asynchronous communications port control:

COMn:baud   "n" represents the asynchronous communications port number, an integer from 1 to 8.

parity

N None. No parity bit.
O Odd. Odd parity.
E Even. Even parity.
M Mark. The parity bit is always 1.
S Space. The parity bit is always 0.

databits   5, 6, 7, or 8 data bits per character are allowed.

stopbits   1, 1.5, or 2 stop bits per character are allowed. When databits=5, stopbits may be either 1 or 1.5. When stopbits=1.5, databits must be 5.

P   Timeout parameter for DOS mode programs that go directly to hardware. It provides a timeout interval of about 30 seconds. The SETCOM40 command must be executed before printing or plotting to tell the program the port address.

TO=state	ON enables "write infinite timeout processing." OFF specifies normal timeout processing.
XON=state	ON enables automatic transmit flow control. OFF disables automatic transmit flow control.
IDSR=state	ON enables input handshaking using Data Set Ready (DSR). OFF disables input handshaking using DSR.
ODSR=state	ON enables output handshaking using DSR. OFF disables output handshaking using DSR.
OCTS=state	ON enables output handshaking using Clear To Send (CTS). OFF disables output handshaking using CTS.
DTR=state	ON enables Data Terminal Ready (DTR). OFF disables DTR. HS enables DTR handshaking.
RTS=state	ON enables Ready to Send (RTS). OFF disables RTS. HS enables RTS handshaking. TOG enables RTS toggling.

In OS/2 mode, every time the MODE command is used to set COM parameters, output handshaking using data carrier detect (DCD) and automatic receive flow control (XON or XOFF) are disabled. In DOS mode, such use of the MODE command does not affect these parameters.

Defaults:

COMn:baud	Default is 1200 baud.
parity	Default is E (even).
databits	Default is 7.
stopbits	Default is 2 when baud is 110. Otherwise default is 1.
P	If not specified, the 30 second timeout is not in effect.
TO=state	Default is OFF.
XON=state	Default is OFF.
IDSR=state	Default is ON.
ODSR=state	Default is ON.
OCTS=state	Default is ON.
DTR=state	Default is ON.
RTS=state	Default is ON.

Exit Codes: None.

Examples: To set your COM1 port to 1200 baud, no parity, 7 data bits and 1 stop bit, issue the command,

```
MODE COM1:12,N,7,1
```

Since most of these values are also defaults, you could have achieved the same effect with the command,

```
MODE COM1:,N,,
```

To query a port for its parameter settings, type

```
MODE COM1
```

The current settings will be displayed on the screen.

Related Command:
  SETCOM40

Syntax: To set display modes:

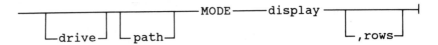

Parameters:

display	40	40 characters per line.
	80	80 characters per line.
	BW40	Color graphics monitor with color disabled, 40 character line.
	BW80	Color graphics monitor with color disabled, 80 character line.
	CO40	Color graphics monitor with color enabled, 40 character line.
	CO80	Color graphics monitor with color enabled, 80 character line.
	MONO	Monochrome monitor, 80 character line.
rows	25	25 rows per screen.
	43	43 rows per screen. Available with EGA.
	50	50 rows per screen. Available with VGA.

NOTE: Each session can independently set its own display mode.

Defaults:

display	With CGA, default is CO80.
	With EGA, default is CO80.
	With VGA, default is CO80.
	With monochrome adapter, default is MONO.
rows	Default is 25.

Exit Codes: None

Examples: To display 43 lines on a VGA display, run the command,

```
MODE C080,43
```

To display 50 lines on the same display, run

```
MODE C080,50
```

To direct the display to a monochrome monitor, issue the command,

```
MODE MONO
```

Syntax: To set parallel printer modes:

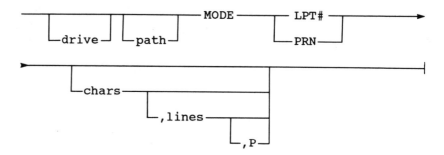

Parameters:

LPT#	# is either 1, 2, or 3. Specifies the printer number.
PRN	An alternate name for LPT1.
chars	Either 80 or 132 characters per line.
lines	Either 6 or 8 lines per inch. Controls the vertical spacing.
P	Causes computer to continue to try to send output to the printer after a timeout error has occurred.

Defaults:

chars	Default is 80.
lines	Default is 6.
P	If P is not specified, system will not continue to try to send output to the printer after a timeout error has occurred.

Exit Codes: None

Remarks: If you specify some parameters and rely on the defaults for others, be sure that you enter commas at the appropriate places to mark the positions of the defaulted parameters. Once you have entered values for parameters, those values become the defaults until they are explicitly changed with another MODE command.

Examples: To set up your primary printer (LPT1) for 132 characters per line, 8 lines per inch, and continue to output after a timeout, issue the following command:

```
MODE PRN 132,8,P
```

Later, to return to 80 characters per line and 6 lines per inch, run another MODE command:

```
MODE PRN 80,6,P
```

To set up a second printer to continue outputting after a timeout, but retain the default values of 80 characters per line and 6 lines per inch, execute

```
MODE LPT2 ,,P
```

Syntax: To set or query diskette I/O write verification:

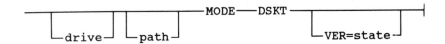

Parameters:

state   ON turns on diskette verification.
            OFF turns off diskette verification.

Default: The default value of "state" is OFF.

Exit Codes: None

Remarks: When you issue the command,

```
MODE DSKT VER=ON
```

all writes done from all sessions to all diskettes are verified. As a result, diskette writes will take longer.

Examples: To query the current status of diskette verification, type

```
MODE DSKT
```

To turn off diskette verification, execute

```
MODE DSKT VER=OFF
```

Related Command:

VERIFY

MORE

Purpose: This filter prevents output sent to the console from being scrolled off the top of the screen. After the screen is full, output pauses until the operator presses a key.

Syntax:

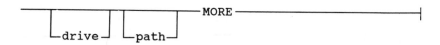

Parameters: None

Default: None

Exit Codes: None

Remarks: The MORE filter can receive input either from a pipe (|) or from a redirected input (<). It sends information to the console, a screenful at a time. At the bottom of the screen it displays the word "—More—". The operator may press any key to display the next screenful. By repeatedly displaying a screenful and pressing a key, the operator can view large files without missing any information. If you have set the display to 43 or 50 lines with the MODE command, MORE will take this into account and display the appropriate number of lines before pausing and displaying the "—More—" message.

MORE stores information temporarily on disk before displaying it. Thus if your disk is almost full or write-protected, the MORE filter will not work properly.

Examples: To display a long ASCII text file on the screen, use syntax like the following:

```
TYPE thesis.txt | MORE
```

The same result could be accomplished using redirection as follows:

```
MORE < thesis.txt
```

Related Commands:
    FIND
    SORT

PATCH

Purpose: Allows the addition of fixes to OS/2 program code.

Syntax:

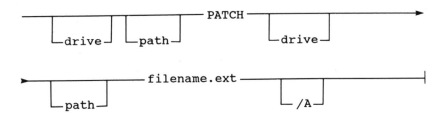

Parameters:

/A   Automatic mode. When this parameter is present, the patching is done automatically. Patches are taken from "filename.ext" and automatically applied to the proper places.

Default: Patches may be applied either automatically or interactively. The default is interactive. In this mode, the operator enters the patches manually from the keyboard.

Exit Codes: None

Remarks: It is virtually impossible to write a large complex software system such as OS/2 without introducing some errors into its code. Recognizing this fact, Microsoft and IBM provide the PATCH command, which allows you to correct such errors. It is a good idea to back up your disk before using the PATCH command. That way, if you do not apply the patches correctly, at least you will be no worse off than you were when you started.

If the patches you have were provided on a diskette that was designed for automatic installation, applying the patch can be a relatively simple procedure. If the patches you have were not configured for automatic installation, you will have to enter them manually from the keyboard. Since the location of the patches (the offset) and the patch code itself must be entered in hexadecimal notation (hex), anyone using PATCH should be familiar with hex.

In interactive mode, when you specify an offset, the 16 bytes starting at the offset location will be displayed on the screen. The cursor will be resting on the first byte. You may change the byte or press the space bar to move on to the next one. In this manner you can proceed through all 16 displayed bytes. If you continue past the sixteenth byte, the next 16 bytes will be displayed.

When you have finished entering the current patch, press Enter. Your changes will be saved. If you have made mistakes and want either to start over or leave things as they were, press Esc. This tells PATCH not to save the changes. In either case, a prompt will ask you if you want to continue patching. If you respond with a "Y", you will be asked for another offset. If you respond with a "N", all the patches that you have made will be displayed and you will be asked to verify that you want to apply the patches. If you reply in the affirmative, the patches will be applied to your disk. If you reply in the negative, no patches will be applied, and you will be returned to the command prompt.

Related Facility:

Microsoft CodeView Debugger

PATH

Purpose: Tells OS/2 where to search for a program or batch file if the file cannot be found in the current directory.

Syntax: The PATH command is used three ways:
1. To specify search paths where program or batch files may be found.
2. To cause a display of the paths that are currently in effect.
3. To remove all paths.

The syntax for each use is slightly different, so we will show three syntax diagrams.

Syntax to specify search paths.

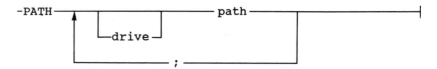

Syntax to display paths currently in effect.

```
PATH ――――――――――――――――――――――――――――――――――――――|
```

Syntax to remove all paths.

```
PATH ―――――――――――――――― ; ―――――――――――――――――|
```

Parameters: None

Default: None

Exit Codes: None

Remarks: PATH is a system environment variable. Paths can be set with the SET command as well as with the PATH command. See the discussion of the SET command.

Several search paths can be specified with a single PATH command. Each path need only be separated from the others by a semicolon. OS/2 searches the paths in the order they are specified in the PATH command. Therefore, it is wise to place the most likely path first and the next most likely second, etc. The less time OS/2 spends searching paths, the more time it spends doing useful work.

The installation program that controls the installation of OS/2 on your hard disk places path commands in the startup batch files "os2init.cmd" and "autoexec.bat". The paths provide access to OS/2 command files, which are used quite often.

If you want to append a new path to an existing PATH command without retyping the whole thing, you can do so by using a replaceable parameter, as follows:

```
PATH %PATH%C:\ws
```

The new path (C:\ws) is added to the existing path, which is represented in the command by %PATH%. This usage will not work unless the original path ends with a semicolon.

If you have an application where program files are kept in one directory and data files are kept in another, you must set up a path between them for the application to function. Make the directory containing the data the current directory. Set a path to the directory containing the program files.

In OS/2 mode you can link directories with paths without regard to where the program files are and where the data files are by using a combination of the PATH command and the DPATH command. In DOS mode you can do the same thing with the PATH command and the APPEND command.

Related Commands:
  APPEND
  DPATH
  SET

PRINT

Purpose: Enables or cancels the printing of one or more files.

Syntax: To enable printing:

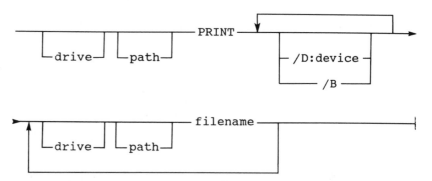

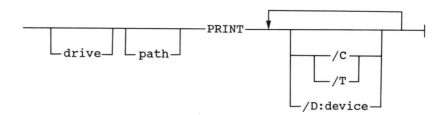

To cancel printing of the current file and any following files in the print queue that are waiting for the specified print device:

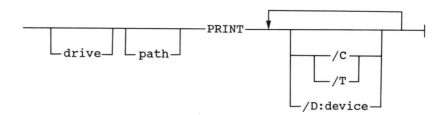

Parameters:

/D:device	Specifies the print device, which may be PRN, LPT1, LPT2, or LPT3.
/B	Causes a Ctrl-Z character to be interpreted literally rather than as an end of file character.
/C	Cancels the printing of the file currently being printed if the SPOOL command is active for the specified device.
/T	Cancels the printing of all files in the print queue if the SPOOL command is active for the specified device.

Default: The default print device is LPT1.

Exit Codes: None

Remarks: As the syntax diagram indicates, the /C and /T parameters cannot be specified with the /B parameter, with a filename, or with each other.

Examples: To print a file, use PRINT in the following manner:

```
PRINT C:\ws\compplan.txt
```

To cancel the print of the currently printing file, use the /C parameter as follows:

```
PRINT /C
```

Related Command:
SPOOL

PROMPT

Purpose: Changes the system command prompt.

Syntax:

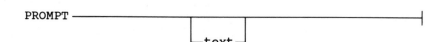

```
PROMPT ─────────────────────────────────────────────────┤
                          └─text─┘
```

Parameters:

text   This may be any text entered from the keyboard and may
            contain one or more prompt parameters. A prompt
            parameter is a dollar sign ($) followed by a letter. The
            following table shows the prompt letters and the
            information they add to the prompt.

Prompt letter	Information added to the prompt
$	The "$" character
—	A carriage return/line feed
A	The "&" character
B	The "|" character
C	The "(" character
D	The current date
E	ASCII code 27 (Esc)
F	The ")" character
G	The ">" character
H	The backspace character
I	The help line
L	The "<" character
N	The default drive
P	The current directory of the default drive
Q	The "=" character
S	A space
T	The current time
V	The OS/2 version number

Default: The default prompt at bootup time in DOS mode is the
default drive, the current directory, followed by the greater-than

character. In subdirectory "\wordproc" on your hard disk, the prompt would look like this:

```
C:\wordproc>
```

If you use the PROMPT command to change the prompt, then try to regain the default prompt by issuing the PROMPT command with no parameters, you will get a new default prompt. This new prompt is just the default drive letter followed by a greater-than sign. To restore the original default prompt you will have to issue the command,

```
PROMPT $p$g
```

In OS/2 mode the default prompt is the default drive, the current directory, enclosed in square brackets. In subdirectory "\rbfiles" on your hard disk, the prompt would appear as follows:

```
[C:\RBFILES]
```

Exit Codes: None:

Remarks: The default prompt in OS/2 mode was intentionally made different from the prompt in DOS mode so you could tell at a glance which mode is currently active. If you decide to change the prompts, it is a good idea to keep them different from each other. When you change the prompt in one session, the prompts in other sessions are unaffected. To maintain consistency, you may want to put PROMPT commands into your "autoexec.bat" file and your "os2init.cmd" file so that all your OS/2 mode sessions will have the same OS/2 mode prompt and your DOS mode session will always have the same DOS mode prompt.

If you have enabled extended keyboard and display support by including a DEVICE=ANSI.SYS statement in your "config.sys" file or by executing the ANSI command, you will be able to include escape sequences in the prompt. With such escape sequences, you can alter various keyboard and video attributes.

The command prompt may also be changed with the SET command. Refer to the coverage of SET later in this chapter.

Example: To remove all prompt characters from the command line and display the help line at the top of the screen, use the I parameter as follows:

```
PROMPT $I
```

To remove all prompt characters from the command line without displaying the help line, use the S and the H parameters:

```
PROMPT $S$H
```

The S parameter changes the prompt to a blank space and advances the cursor to column two. The H parameter backs the cursor up to column one.

Related Commands:
ANSI
DATE
SET
TIME
VER

RECOVER

Purpose: Recovers the undamaged portion of a file or disk that contains bad sectors.

Syntax:

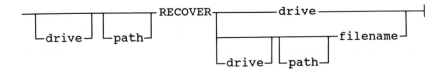

Parameters:

drive   A disk whose directory has been damaged.

filename   A file containing at least one bad sector.

Default: None

Exit Codes: None

Remarks: If you are having trouble accessing information from a disk, it is possible that the disk has been damaged in some way. Use the CHKDSK command to check for disk errors. If you find errors, some but not all of the information on the disk may be recoverable. After a disk has been damaged, RECOVER can be used to salvage any undamaged information. If the directory of the disk has been damaged, use the "RECOVER drive" form of the command to retrieve all the undamaged files. If a particular file on the disk has been damaged, use the "RECOVER filename" form to recover the undamaged portions of the file.

The RECOVER command cannot be used with any drives that have been substituted or joined.

Examples: To recover a damaged file named "document.txt" from a diskette inserted in drive A, issue the command,

```
RECOVER A:\document.txt
```

All data residing in undamaged sectors will be recovered. The data that had been in the damaged sector or sectors is unrecoverable. The same procedure can be used to recover a file from a damaged hard disk.

To recover files from a diskette whose directory has been damaged, use the syntax,

```
RECOVER A:
```

A new root directory will be built, and recovered files will be placed in it under new names. To determine which of your old files have been recovered, you will have to examine the contents of each with the TYPE command or a disk utility program.

Related Command:
    CHKDSK

RENAME (REN)

Purpose: Changes the name of a disk file.

Syntax:

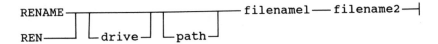

Parameters:

filename1   Specifies one or more files whose names will be changed.

filename2   Specifies the new names for the files.

Default: None

Exit Codes: None

Remarks: Wildcards (? or *) may be used in either the source or the destination filename. If used in the source filename, all filenames in the specified directory that match the specified ambiguous filename will be changed. If wildcards are used in the destination filename, all character positions occupied by a wildcard will *not* be changed.

Either RENAME or the shortened form REN may be used interchangeably.

Examples: To rename a diary file named "current.txt" to "march88.txt", type

```
RENAME C:\wordproc\current.txt march88.txt
```

If you were an author about to embark on his or her second novel, who already had files named, "novelch1.txt", "novelch2.txt", "novelch3.txt", . . . , you would probably want to rename them as follows:

```
RENAME C:\wordproc\novel*.txt book1*.txt
```

This would change "novelch1.txt" to "book1ch1.txt", "novelch2.txt" to "book1ch2.txt", and so on. You are now ready to start writing "book2ch1.txt" without fear of getting the chapters of your two books mixed up.

Related Command:
    COPY

REPLACE

Purpose: Replaces files on the target drive with files of the same name on the source drive. Also can be used to add files from the source drive that do not exist on the target drive.

Syntax:

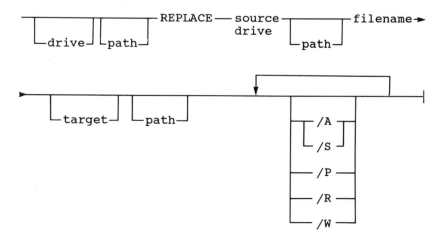

Parameters:

None	Replaces files only in the specified directory of the target disk.
/A	Adds new files to the target directory instead of replacing existing files. This parameter may not be used together with the /S parameter.
/S	Searches all subdirectories of the target disk for matches to the source file specification. Replaces matching files with their counterparts from the source disk.
/P	Prompts you as it finds each match. You are given the opportunity to select which matching files to replace and which to leave unchanged.
/R	Enables the replacement of read-only files on the target disk as well as read/write files.
/W	Waits for you to insert a diskette before proceeding with the replace operation.

Default: Copies the file or files specified on the source drive over the top of files with the same name in the current directory of the target drive.

Exit Codes:

0   Command successful.

2   File not found.

3   Path not found.

5   Access code for reading and writing is not correct.
        Try again, specifying the /R parameter.

8   Not enough memory.

11   Invalid command line format.

15   Invalid drive.

22   Unknown command.

Remarks: The REPLACE command provides a convenient means for you to update an application system on your hard disk with the latest release of the same package. Updated files on the source diskette replace older equivalents on the hard disk. If any new files are present on the source disk, you can add them by performing REPLACE again, specifying the /A parameter.

Hidden files and system files are not affected by the REPLACE command.

Examples: You have just received the latest version of the language interpreter "basica.com" on a diskette. You have several copies of an older release of the file in various subdirectories of your hard disk. To replace them all with the new version, type

```
REPLACE A:\basica.com C:\ /S /W
```

The /W parameter will pause the operation to give you a chance to insert the source floppy into drive A. The /S parameter will cause all subdirectories in drive C to be searched for files named "basica.com". Whenever such a file is found, it is replaced with the file from drive A.

Related Commands:
   COPY
   XCOPY

RESTORE

Purpose: Restores files that were backed up using the BACKUP command.

Syntax:

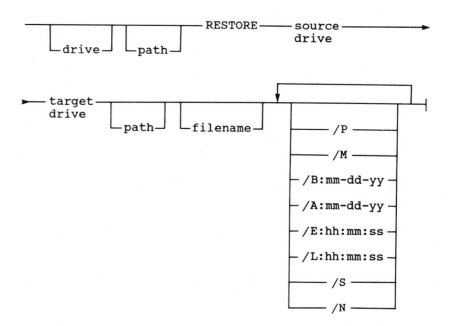

Parameters:

/P	Prompts for confirmation to restore over files on the target disk that are read-only or that have been updated since the backup was made.
/M	Restores only the files on the target disk that have been modified since the last backup.
/B:mm–dd–yy	Restores only those files on the target disk that were modified on or before the specified date.
/A:mm–dd–yy	Restores only those files on the target disk that were modified on or after the specified date.
/E:hh:mm:ss	Restores only those files on the target disk that were modified at or earlier than the specified time.
/L:hh:mm:ss	Restores only those files on the target disk that were modified at or later than the specified time.

/S   Restores any subdirectories from the backup disk
                 to the target disk, if they do not exist on the
                 target disk.

/N   Restores any files from the backup disk to the
                 target disk that do not exist on the target disk.

Default: Restores the files on the source disk to the target disk. Files will be restored only to subdirectories that already exist on the target disk. RESTORE will not create subdirectories on the target disk unless the /S parameter is specified.

Exit Codes:

0   Normal completion.

1   No files were found to restore.

2   Some files not restored due to sharing error.

3   Terminated by user.

Remarks: Just as you can back up from any kind of drive to any kind of drive, you can also restore from any kind of drive to any kind of drive. The *source drive* is the drive containing the backup files. The *target drive* is the device to which you want to restore the files. Wildcards can be used in specifying the target filename. All files matching the ambiguous filename will be restored.

   RESTORE does not affect the system commands. To transfer "ibmbio.com" and "ibmdos.com", you must use the SYS command. To transfer the "command.com" and "cmd.exe" files, you must use the COPY command.

Examples: The most common use of RESTORE is to restore a complete backup from floppy diskettes to a hard disk. To perform this operation, use

```
RESTORE A: C:\*.* /S
```

Of course, this assumes that a complete backup had previously been made using the BACKUP command, with the syntax

```
BACKUP C:\*.* A:/S
```

Related Commands:
   ATTRIB
   BACKUP

RMDIR

Purpose: Removes empty subdirectories from a disk.

Syntax:

[D]

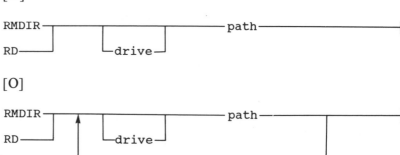

[O]

Parameters:

path   The path specifies the subdirectory to be removed.

Default: None

Exit Codes: None

Remarks: A directory must be empty before it can be removed. It must contain no files and have no subdirectories. If a directory contains one or more hidden files, the DIR command will indicate that the directory is empty. However, the RMDIR command will not remove the directory. You must first delete the hidden files before the directory can be removed.

The root directory cannot be removed, nor can the current directory. If the current directory is empty and you wish to remove it, change directories with the CHDIR command to any other directory, then remove the empty directory.

The RMDIR command cannot be used on drives that are substituted or joined. Either the full command name RMDIR or its shorter form RD may be used interchangeably.

In OS/2 mode, it is possible to remove several directories with a single command. Just specify the directories to be removed, one after the other.

Example: You have taken a large data base management system off of your hard disk to free up some room. Now to remove the empty directory, issue the command

```
RD C:\dbase
```

In OS/2 mode, you have erased all records pertaining to a company you have just sold, Acme, Inc. To remove all the empty directories from your hard disk and from an associated floppy disk, type

`RMDIR C:\acmeacct C:\acmewp C:\acmesale A:\acmedata`

Related Commands:
CHDIR
DIR
MKDIR
TREE

SET

Purpose: Displays or assigns values to environment variables.

Syntax:

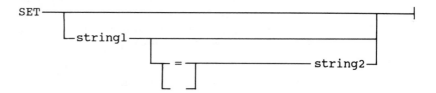

Parameters:

None	Display the environment.
string1	The name of a system or environment variable or a replaceable parameter.
string2	The value to be assigned to the system variable or replaceable parameter. String1 and string2 may be separated by either an equal sign or a blank space, but not by both.

Default: If no parameters are specified, OS/2 displays the environment. All environment variables are shown, along with their values.

Exit Codes: None

Remarks: To create a new environment variable, specify both string1 and string2. OS/2 will create an environment variable named string1 and set it equal to string2. To change the value of an existing environment variable, specify the variable as string1 and specify the new value as string2. To remove a variable from the environment, specify the variable as string1 and do not specify string2.

In addition to variables that you create, the environment may also contain system variables and replaceable parameters. System variables are commands such as DPATH, PATH, and PROMPT, as well as other variables such as COMSPEC. COMSPEC specifies where in the directory tree the system files are located.

Batch files, as well as application programs, can make use of information stored in environment variables to affect program execution. You may wish to SET environment variables in your "autoexec.bat" and "os2init.cmd" files. They would establish your desired environment at system startup, and remain in effect until changed by subsequent SET commands.

Examples: The SET command becomes a powerful tool when combined with replaceable parameters. Suppose you want to print status information about your business every month. Rather than typing the needed commands every time, create a batch file utilizing replaceable parameters to do the job automatically. First create a batch file with one or more commands containing the replaceable parameter. For example,

```
PRINT %statrpt%
```

Next create the associated environment variable as follows:

```
SET statrpt=april.rpt
```

When the batch file is executed, OS/2 will substitute "april.rpt" for the replaceable parameter "%statrpt%". The following month, you need only issue the command,

```
SET statrpt=may.rpt
```

Whenever "%statrpt%" occurs in a batch file or program file, it will now be replaced by the new value "may.rpt". In this manner, you need change only one variable rather than multiple occurrences scattered throughout several files.

Replaceable parameters can also be used with the PROMPT and PATH system variables. Say your "os2init.cmd" file has set a path as follows:

```
PATH=C:\;C:\OS2;C:\OS2\INSTALL;
```

You want to add your word processing directory to the path but don't want to retype the entire command. Use a replaceable parameter with the SET command:

```
SET PATH=%PATH%C:\wordproc;
```

OS/2 substitutes the original path for the replaceable parameter %PATH%, then adds on the new addition (C:\wordproc). For this method to work, the last character of the original path must be a semicolon.

Replaceable parameters can also be used by the APPEND, DPATH, PATH, and PROMPT commands. For example, we could accomplish the same result achieved above with the command,

```
PATH %PATH%C:\wordproc;
```

Note that the syntax of the SET PATH and the PATH commands are different, even though they both have the same result. Be sure to use the appropriate syntax for each command.

Related Commands:
APPEND
DPATH
PATH
PROMPT

[D] SETCOM40

Purpose: Allows DOS mode programs to directly access a COM port rather than going through the OS/2 serial port driver.

Syntax:

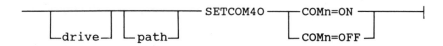

Parameters:

COMn	COM1, COM2, or COM3
ON	Sets the port address for a serial device.
OFF	Removes the port address.

Default: None

Exit Codes: None

Remarks: Programs that were originally written for IBM Personal Computer DOS or Microsoft MS-DOS may access one of your serial ports directly, rather than going through the appropriate "com0x.sys" device driver. To accommodate such programs, set the port address ON. This takes control of the serial port away from OS/2. For this reason, the SETCOM40 command should not be used to set ON a serial port that is also being used by another process through the "com0x.sys" driver.

Examples: To run an MS-DOS program that uses serial port COM1, execute

```
SETCOM40 COM1=ON
```

After you have run the MS-DOS application, to protect the system from possible conflicts with protected mode applications using the "com01.sys" device driver, issue the command,

```
SETCOM40 COM1=OFF
```

Related Command:
    DEVICE=com0x.sys statement in "config.sys"

SORT

Purpose: Reads input from the standard input device, sorts it, then writes it to the standard output device.

Syntax:

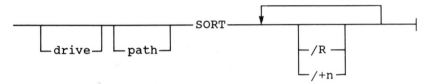

Parameters:

/R   Reverses the sort to descending order rather than ascending order.

/+n   Begins the sort at column n of each input line.

Defaults: The default sort order is ascending. The default column to start sorting on is column 1. The default standard input device is the keyboard, and the default standard output device is the video screen.

Exit Codes: None

Remarks: The SORT filter may receive input from a pipe, or it may receive redirected input from a file. Similarly, it may send output to a pipe or send redirected output to a file. Normally, it receives input from the keyboard and sends output to the video screen.

SORT treats upper case and lower case letters as being the same. Thus "almond" would be located close to "ALMOND", rather than being after "Zanzibar". Characters above ASCII 127 are treated differently depending on which country code has been selected.

Examples: You can sort a directory and view the result one screenful at a time with

```
DIR | SORT | MORE
```

To sort by extension rather than by filename, use the /+n parameter:

```
DIR | SORT /+10 | MORE
```

Since the file extension starts in column 10, the resulting display will be sorted by extension.

To sort an invoice data file in reverse alphabetical order, type

```
SORT /R < invoice.dta
```

Related Commands:

CODEPAGE statement in "config.sys"

COUNTRY statement in "config.sys"

[O] SPOOL

Purpose: Controls background printing of material from multiple sources, keeping each job separate.

Syntax:

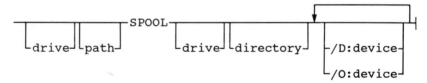

Parameters: The drive and directory parameters after the SPOOL command specify the location of the print spool subdirectory. Temporary spool files will be placed here before they are sent to the printer.

/D:device   Specifies the input print device. This is the device to which the application thinks it is printing. LPT1, LPT2, LPT3, and PRN are the only permissible devices.

/O:device   Specifies the output print device. This is the device to which the spooled output will actually be directed. COM1, COM2, and COM3 may be specified as well as the parallel ports permitted for the input print device. To output to a serial port, the corresponding serial device driver (com0x.sys) must be present in the "config.sys" file.

Defaults: The default print spool directory is "\spool".

The default input print device is LPT1.

The default output print device is the same as the input print device.

Exit Codes: None

Remarks: The spooler intercepts and sorts data being sent by multiple processes to the printer. Rather than having the data from concurrently running processes intermixed on the printer, each print job is maintained in a separate temporary spool file until it is complete. At that time it is placed in a print queue and each job is printed out sequentially.

The "\spool" directory is set up at system installation time, and the normal "os2init.cmd" batch file starts the spooler running by executing the SPOOL command. Since the spooler does not require any operator intervention, it can operate in the background.

If your printer has a serial interface, you can use it by setting up your application software as if it were using a parallel printer such as LPT1. The spooler will accept input directed to a parallel input print device. Make sure that you have a DEVICE=com01.sys statement in your "config.sys" file and specify COM1 as the output print device in your SPOOL command. You may also have to specify serial port parameters such as baud rate and parity, with a MODE command.

Most DOS mode programs were not designed to work with the spooler. They do not signal the spooler as to when to start printing. As a result, printing will not commence until you exit the application. You can cause printing to begin without exiting the application by pressing Ctrl-Alt-PrtSc. You must make sure that the entire file to be printed has been completely processed and sent to the print queue before you press Ctrl-Alt-PrtSc. If you start the print too soon, your job will be printed in two segments.

It is possible to direct output to multiple printers by starting multiple spoolers running. Each printer would have its own spooler.

Examples: The standard system installation assumes a parallel printer connected to the first parallel printer port (LPT1). The spooler is invoked with the command,

```
RUN=C:\OS2\SPOOL.EXE
```

The default input print device is LPT1, and the default output print device is the same as the input device. In this case, it is LPT1.

To send output to a serial printer connected to the COM2 port, issue the command,

```
RUN=C:\OS2\SPOOL.EXE /D:LPT2 /O:COM2
```

Even though there is nothing physically connected to the LPT2 port, output is properly directed to the serial printer on COM2.

If the spooler is active, to cancel the printing of files in the print queue you must use the PRINT command with the /T or the /C parameter.

Related Commands:
MODE
PRINT
SETCOM40

[O] START

Purpose: Starts an OS/2 mode program in another session.

Syntax:

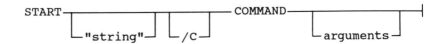

Parameters:

string   The program title, which will appear on the Program
           Selector menu. The string must be enclosed in double
           quotes and must be 30 characters or less in length.

/C   Terminates the session when the specified command
           is completed. When the session is terminated, either
           another session or the Program Selector menu is
           displayed on the screen.

command   An OS/2 command, a ".cmd" batch file or an OS/2
           program that you want to pass to the new OS/2
           command processor you are starting.

Default: If a "string" is not specified, the filename of the file being started is used in its place. If the START command is issued with no parameters, an OS/2 command processor is started.

Exit Codes: None

Remarks: The START command is primarily used to start programs automatically at system startup. It can also be invoked at any time from the OS/2 command prompt. You can create a special startup batch file named "startup.cmd". If OS/2 finds such a file in the root directory at system startup time, it will automatically execute the commands in that file. In this way you can go directly into an application, rather than displaying the Program Selector Menu.

Examples: If sixty to eighty percent of your computer usage is word processing, you may want to boot directly into your word processor. You could do it by putting the following commands into your "startup.cmd" file:

```
CD \wordproc
START "Start Word Processor" WORD
```

A new session is started, and the word processing application is activated. You can switch at any time to the Program Selector Menu by pressing Ctrl-Esc. Since you did not specify the /C parameter, the session will not end when you exit from the word processor. Control will be returned to the session command prompt.

Related Commands:
CMD
STARTUP.CMD autostart batch file

[D] SUBST

Purpose: Substitutes a drive letter for a drive and path specification, creating a virtual drive.

Syntax: To substitute a drive letter for another drive and path:

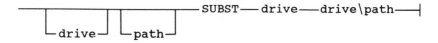

To display substitutions currently in effect:

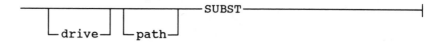

To delete substitutions currently in effect:

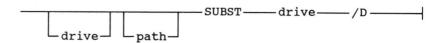

Parameters:

None	Display substitutions currently in effect.
drive	The drive letter that is to be substituted. The identifier of the new virtual drive.
drive \ path	The drive and path to be reidentified.
/D	Delete a substituted drive.

Default: None

Exit Codes: None

Remarks: SUBST can be used to provide a shorthand designation for a frequently used directory that is at the end of a long path specification.

Drive substitution is not compatible with the following OS/2 commands:

CHKDSK
DISKCOPY
FDISK
FORMAT
LABEL

RECOVER
SYS

Do not use any of these commands on a substituted drive.

Examples: This command creates a short drive designation for a directory buried deeply in a hard disk directory tree:

`SUBST E: C:\acmecorp\acctng\receivab\delinq`

You can now directly access files in the delinquent account directory by asking for drive E.

Delete the substituted drive with

`SUBST E: /D`

Related Commands:
JOIN
ASSIGN

SYS

Purpose: Transfers the OS/2 hidden system files from the default drive to the specified drive.

Syntax:

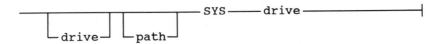

Parameters:

drive The hidden system files "ibmbio.com" and "ibmdos.com" are transferred onto this drive, making it bootable.

Default: None

Exit Codes: None

Remarks: The specified drive must either be a newly formatted hard disk, a newly formatted diskette, or it must already contain hidden system files as the first two directory entries. Since the OS/2 versions of "ibmbio.com" and "ibmdos.com" are smaller than the corresponding files for IBM PC-DOS, you can copy the OS/2 system onto bootable DOS disks without having to reformat them.

System files which are not hidden are not transferred by the SYS command. You will need to use the COPY command to transfer such files as "command.com", "cmd.exe", etc. All needed files are specified in the file "formats.tbl."

Do not use SYS when ASSIGN, JOIN, or SUBST is in effect for the drive you are transferring to.

Example: To copy OS/2 system files to a newly formatted hard disk, issue the command,

    SYS C:

To make an old IBM PC-DOS boot diskette bootable under OS/2, issue

    SYS A:

Related Command:
    FORMAT

TIME

Purpose: Displays or changes the time known to the system.

Syntax:

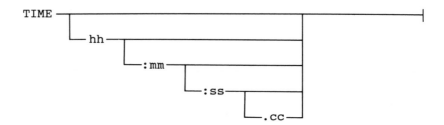

Parameters:

hh   hours. Must be 0 to 23.

mm   minutes. Must be 0 to 59.

ss   seconds. Must be 0 to 59.

cc   hundredths of a second. Must be 0 to 99.

The parameters are separated by the delimiters specified by the COUNTRY command.

Default: The U.S. separator between hours and minutes, and between minutes and seconds is the colon. Between seconds and hundredths of a second, the U.S. separator is the decimal point. In other countries, see the country-dependent information file for the corresponding separators.

Exit Codes: None

Remarks: Time is displayed and entered in the 24-hour format. If you enter the TIME command with no parameters, the current system time is displayed, and you are asked to enter the new time. If you do not want to change the time, press the Enter key. To change the time, enter the new time in 24 hour format.

Examples: If you enter
```
    TIME
```
OS/2 responds
```
    The current time is hh:mm:ss.cc
    Enter the new time:_
```
The time that you enter at this point becomes the new time kept by the system. Whenever files are created or modified, they are time stamped with the current time.

You can accomplish the same result in a single step by specifying the new time in the TIME command, as follows:

    TIME 09:30

In this case, since only hours and minutes were specified, seconds and hundredths of a second are set to zero.

Related Commands:
    COUNTRY statement in "config.sys"
    DATE
    PROMPT

[O] TRACE

Purpose: Enables and disables the tracing of system events for fault diagnosis.

Syntax:

Parameters:

ON   Enables system tracing of specified events.

OFF   Disables system tracing of specified events.

x   Event code. A number between 0 and 255.

Default: The default is TRACE OFF.

Exit Codes: None

Remarks: Events that can be monitored by TRACE include such operations as the opening of a file, writing to a file, and sending output to a display. The event code numbers are maintained by IBM Service Representatives and do not appear in normal OS/2 user documentation. If no major event code is specified, then all events will be traced.

The TRACE command will not work and an error message will be issued unless system trace information is present in the "config.sys" file.

Related Commands:

    TRACE statement in "config.sys"
    TRACEBUF statement in "config.sys"
    TRACEFMT

[O] TRACEFMT

Purpose: Displays formatted trace records in reverse time stamp order.

Syntax:

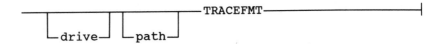

Parameters: None

Default: Formats and displays the contents of the system trace buffer.

Exit Codes: None

Remarks: The system events captured by the TRACE command are stored in the trace buffer set up by the TRACEBUF statement in the "config.sys" file. The TRACEFMT command takes those records and formats them for display on the video screen. This display can be redirected to a printer or to a file.

Example: To dump the contents of the trace buffer to your system printer, issue the command,

```
TRACEFMT > LPT1
```

Related Commands:
TRACE statement in "config.sys"
TRACEBUF statement in "config.sys"
TRACE

TREE

Purpose: Displays all the subdirectories on a disk and optionally displays the names of all the files in the root directory and all the subdirectories.

Syntax:

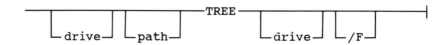

Parameters:

/F   Causes filenames to be displayed as well as directory names.

Default: If no drive is specified, the TREE operation is performed on the default drive. If /F is not specified, only the directory names are displayed.

Exit Codes: None

Remarks: The TREE command is not particularly useful for visualizing the organization of the directories. Only a small portion of the tree is shown in any one screenful. To keep the TREE display from scrolling off the top of the screen faster than you can read it, you may want to use the MORE filter.

Examples: To display the directory tree of your hard disk, pausing long enough for you to read it, use the command line,

```
TREE | MORE
```
To print the complete tree, including all filenames, type
```
TREE /F > LPT1
```

Related Commands:
CHDIR
DIR
MKDIR
RMDIR

TYPE

Purpose: Displays the contents of the specified file on the screen.

Syntax:

[D]

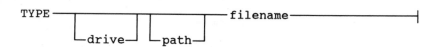

[O]

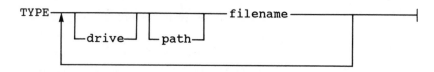

Parameters: None

Default: None

Exit Codes: None

Remarks: TYPE displays a file without allowing modifications. If the file contains tab characters, in the display they are expanded to the current setting for tabs, which is usually 8 characters.

In OS/2 mode, multiple files can be specified with a single TYPE command. If a specified filename contains wildcard characters, each file that matches the ambiguous filename is displayed, just as if they had been separately listed.

Examples: To display an ASCII text file, use syntax like the following:

```
TYPE rufdraft.txt
```

This method will work equally well in displaying OS/2 command files or other uncompiled program files:

```
TYPE os2init.cmd
```

In OS/2 mode you can display the contents of several files with a command similar to this:

```
TYPE C:\wordproc\memo1.txt C:\spread\budget88.wks A:setup.cmd
```

Related Command:

MORE

VER

Purpose: Displays the version number of the OS/2 being used.

Syntax:

```
VER ──────────────────────────────────────────────────────┤
```

Parameters: None

Default: None

Exit Codes: None

Remarks: Application software that is compatible with one version of an operating system is not always compatible with another version. To verify that the version of OS/2 that resides on your system will work with your application, make a quick check of your OS/2 version with the VER command.

Example: To verify the version number of OS/2, issue the command,
```
VER
```
OS/2 will respond with a message like the following:
```
The IBM Operating System/2 Version
   is 1.00
```

Related Command:
```
PROMPT
```

VERIFY

Purpose: Verifies that data written to disk has been written correctly.

Syntax:

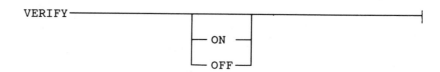

Parameters:

None   Displays current status of the verify parameter.

ON   Enables the verification of all write operations to the default disk.

OFF   Disables the verification of all write operations to the default disk.

Default: The default condition is VERIFY OFF.

Exit Codes: None

Remarks: When verification is ON, OS/2 will notify you of any failed write operations with an error message. This could be of great value in preserving important data. Conversely, when verification is OFF, write operations take place significantly faster. If some of your write operations are particularly important, for example a disk backup, you may wish to set VERIFY ON and suffer the accompanying performance degradation. The rest of the time you can run with VERIFY OFF and operate at full speed.

Once the state of the VERIFY parameter has been changed, it remains in the new state until it is changed again with another VERIFY command or with a SET VERIFY command.

Examples: To check whether VERIFY is ON or OFF, issue the command without a parameter, like this:

    VERIFY

OS/2 will display the message:

    VERIFY is off.

To set verification on, use the following syntax:

    VERIFY ON

Now if you issue the VERIFY command without a parameter, OS/2 will display:

    VERIFY is on.

Related Commands:
    COPY /V
    MODE DSKT
    XCOPY /V

VOL

Purpose: Displays the disk volume label (volume ID) if it exists.

Syntax:

[D]

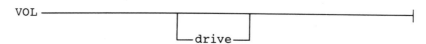

[O]

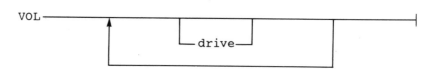

Parameters: None

Default: If you do not specify a drive, OS/2 will display the volume label of the default drive.

Remarks: In OS/2 mode you may specify more than one drive. The VOL command will cause the labels of all specified drives to be displayed consecutively.

Examples: To display the volume label of your hard disk, issue the command,

```
VOL C:
```
OS/2 will display a message similar to the following:
```
The volume label in drive C is OS2.
```
To check the volume labels of multiple disks in OS/2 mode, issue a command like
```
VOL C: A:
```
OS/2 will display
```
The volume in drive C is OS2.
Volume in drive A has no label.
```
OS/2 reports the fact that the diskette inserted into drive A has not been given a label.

Related Commands:
FORMAT
LABEL

XCOPY

Purpose: Copies files and subdirectories from one disk location to another.

Syntax:

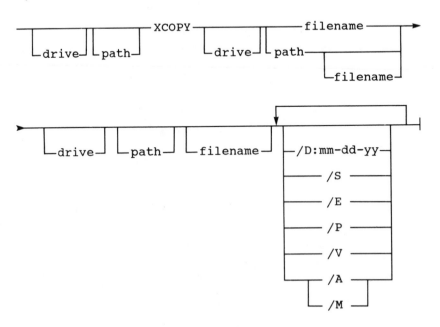

Parameters:

/D:mm–dd–yy	Copies files that were modified on or after the specified date.
/S	Copies subdirectories of the specified directory. Does not cause the copying of empty subdirectories.
/E	When used with the /S parameter, causes the entire directory tree to be copied. Even empty subdirectories are included.
/P	Prompts the operator with "(Y/N)?" before each file is copied, allowing selective copying.
/V	Verifies that data has been correctly written on the target disk.
/A	Copies only archive files, but does not affect the state of the source file's archive bit.
/M	Copies only archive files and turns off the archive bit on the source file. Since the BACKUP

command also uses the archive bit, care must be taken when using both BACKUP and XCOPY /M.

Default: If no parameters are specified, XCOPY copies the files specified in the source filespec to the location given in the target filespec.

Exit Codes:

0   Successful copy.

1   No files were found to copy.

2   Ctrl-C was entered by the operator to terminate the copy operation.

4   Initialization error. Due to:
        Insufficient memory
        Invalid drive
        Invalid command line syntax
        File not found
        Path not found

5   "Int 24" error. Operator aborted operation while reading from or writing to disk.

Remarks: XCOPY copies files or an entire directory (including its subdirectories) from a source file specification to a target file specification. If you are copying files, XCOPY acts much like COPY. The file or files in the source specification are copied to the location given by the target specification.

    If you are copying directories, XCOPY copies all the files in the source directory into the target directory. If you specify a target directory that does not yet exist, XCOPY will create it for you, then copy the source files into it.

Examples: Suppose you have two drives whose directory trees have the following structure:

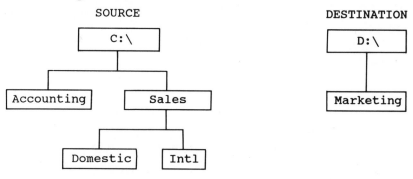

To copy all the files related to Sales onto the same disk with the Marketing files, use the following command:

```
XCOPY C:\sales\ D:\sales\ /s
```

Since the "\sales" subdirectory does not yet exist on drive D, XCOPY creates it, then copies all sales files, including the "\sales\domestic" and "\sales\intl" subdirectories into the newly created directory. The resulting structure looks like the following:

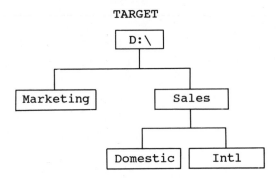

If you were to issue the command,

```
XCOPY C:\sales\ D:\ /s
```

XCOPY would copy the files in the "\sales" directory of drive C into the root directory of drive D. The "\domestic" and "\intl" directories would become subdirectories of the root directory on drive D. The resulting structure would be

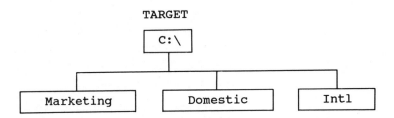

Related Commands:
  BACKUP
  COPY
  VERIFY

Index